DEVIL'S DANDRUFF

GUIDE TO NIGHTLIFE

First published in 2005 by
Gerald Duckworth & Co. Ltd
90-93 Cowcross Street, London EC1M 6BF
Tel: 020 7490 7300
Fax: 020 7490 0080
inquiries@duckworth-publishers.co.uk
www.ducknet.co.uk

A catalogue record for this book is available
from the British Library

ISBN 0-7156-3465-8

Book design by phil.seddon&fiorella.lee@thingsworthseeing.com

Printed in China through Printworks Int. Ltd

DUCKWORTH

DEVIL'S DANDRUFF

GUIDE TO NIGHTLIFE

By Neil Boorman & Daniel Pemberton
Illustrations by Elliot Thoburn

FOREWORD

This illustrated encyclopaedia is the result of ten year's extensive research in the field of British club culture. The habits, generalisations, stereotypes and catch-alls detailed herein are based upon countless hours waiting in queues at the bogs, being insulted by bouncers, ignored by DJs and turned down by the opposite sex.

The common objectives for those participating in club culture are relatively simple to identify, but surprisingly difficult to achieve. Dancing to agreeable music, reaching a state of intoxication/euphoria and engaging with attractive people would appear to be simple goals in confined spaces with loud music, plentiful drink/drugs and five hundred half naked young adults. Yet the unending quest for a repeat experience of 'the perfect night out' is something which both undermines and perpetuates the culture as a whole. In laymen's terms, club culture is routinely shit, but worth repeating in case it gets less so. And it still beats staying in and watching late night telly. Just.

CONTENTS

PART 1: PRE-CLUB
THE CALM BEFORE THE STORM

Hours in front of the makeup mirror, euphoric dancing in the bedroom to party classics, early drinks in the boozer waiting for the 'extras' to turn up; the initial build-up to a night's clubbing is a frenetic mix of preening, posturing, rabble rousing and inflated expectations... often the most exciting part of the night.

PART 2: ARRIVING
THE CARNAGE COMMENCES

Finally arriving at the venue, a series of obstacles must be negotiated in order to start having fun; the blaggers, the bouncers, the guestlist, and the never ending queue. Convoluted rituals must be performed before one can 'enjoy' the overhyped, overpriced and oversubscribed delights inside.

PART 3: ON THE DANCEFLOOR
IMMORAL UTOPIA...
WITH FLASHING LIGHTS

Sexually active youths plus mind altering substances multiplied by hedonistic abandon equals big night out... as long as the DJ plays stuff you can dance to, the bar service is snappy, the pill peaks outnumber the troughs and no throws up over your shoes. No mean feat.

PART 4: POST DISCO
THE ALMIGHTY COMEDOWN

The confused journey back to planet earth, then home. As the club turfs out, the party is momentarily over, and the bun fight for transport, sustenance and one more place to boogie ensues. A terrifying sight to early morning dog walkers.

Why Clubbers Go Clubbing

The uninitiated may believe that the attending of discotheques is purely for the purposes of dancing and socialising to loud music. From extensive field research, this has been disproved, as this diagram explains.

21% Taking drugs
Getting over-excited at the pre-club bar and necking all the pills. Peaking in the queue. Monging out by the fire escape.

14% Buying drugs
Giving dodgy looking strangers hard earned cash and complete trust in regards to your physical and mental health in exchange for three Pro Plus tablets and a bag of banana peelings.

5% Selling drugs
The vending of Pro Plus and banana peels to freshmen students, bribing of bouncers and wearing of cheap sportswear.

10% Actually listening to new music
Only noticing a record when the breakdown kicks in and everyone else has stopped dancing. Looking lost, then punching the air then bouncing around for a while when the beat comes back.

12% Posing
Dancing suggestively with same sex friend while looking over at you (girls) or flexing/ rubbing tricep muscles in a tight t-shirt (boys).

10% Only place still open selling booze
A tricky choice between the 24hr snooker club (certain death) and the late night club (certain boredom). Either way, the cans of Wife Beater are warmer than the atmosphere behind the bar.

25% Misguided expectation of sexual copulation
Hours of preening, shaving, shopping, ironing and exercising are spent preparing for this one act of casual affection, which in reality happens (a) all the time but with ugly brutes (girls/ gays) or (b) once in a blue moon when the kebab breath isn't so strong (boys).

3% Thought it was a cinema
Oh, I came for the new Richard Curtis rom-com and a value bag of Revels. Can you tell me where the exit is please, there's been a mistake.

MOTIVATIONS TO MOSH

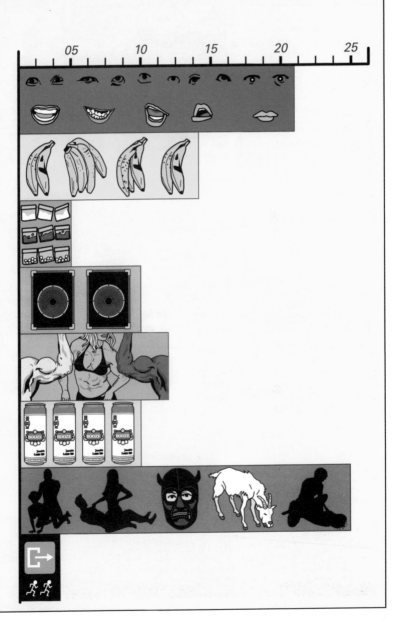

Disco Transport

For club species aware of nightlife's deeply shallow nature, the impact of arrival on a long queue of excited and impressionable contemporaries is an art form in itself. Modes of transport are crucial building blocks in the status of a punter, and can dictate the success rate of entry, back-slapping among mates and the pulling of members of the opposite sex.

Walking

Wow Factor: 5
Gives off the impression that you live within minutes of the venue. Good for venues located in a swanky part of town. Not so good when they are located next to a pig rendering plant in the middle of an industrial trading estate.

Speed/ Safety: 3
Depends on your route. Along well-policed high street – high. Shortcut through local estate full of yellow boards saying 'INCIDENT – CAN YOU HELP?'- low.

Damage: 2
Wear and tear on the Reebok Classics is marginal. Not recommended for girls in high heels over long distances unless on first name terms with local chiropractor.

Entertainment: 2
The chance to absorb all that nature has to offer and mentally reflect on your purpose in life made slightly harder by overpowering stench of kebab meat and chicken fat from nearby takeaway.

Motorised Push Scooter

Wow Factor: 7
Depends on the 'wow' factor you're after. If it's the 'wow what a prick' type then this is your baby. If not then avoid.

Speed/ Safety: 2
Marginally speedier than walking, but you become a target for every 13 year old with an ASBO to throw full cans of Super T at.

Damage: 3
The journey itself is cheap as chips. Having to buy a new scooter the next day because you didn't lock it up properly however is usually more costly.

Entertainment: 4
Good for polishing up your verbal sparring skills with the local population.

Rickshaw

Wow Factor: 3
Unless you're attending an illegal trance do in a cave, or some new tofu-orientated disco, this is social suicide. Wear a hat, sunglasses and cape.

Speed/ Safety: 2
A crazed Aussie traveller seeing double on mushrooms, peddling ten to the dozen on a busy main road? Fare should come with insurance.

Damage: 9
Physical slavery comes cheap, especially when the driver's Shroom psychosis is on a high.

Entertainment: 5
Peddle-powered radio pumps Trance FM's progressive didgeridoo hits into the passenger seat.

DEVIL'S TRUMPS

Bus

Wow factor: 2
They say that when you step out of a limo you feel like a million dollars. When you step off the bus you feel more like a pocket of loose change totalling less than £1.17. No posing value whatsoever.

Speed/ Safety: 8
Unless it's trainee driver day and they've decided to take you on a scenic route of low level bridges then you're in pretty safe hands.

Damage: 1
A beleaguered overworked driver is every tight arse's godsend; either sneak in on the back or confidently flash your local video shop members card for another public transport freebie.

Entertainment: 2
Unless there's a drunk tramp on board things don't get much more boring than sitting with thirty seven people all fastidiously avoiding eye contact for half an hour.

Mini Cab

Wow Factor: 5
A large bang goes off in the night and the entire queue turns round to see. Is it a gun fight? A clap of thunder? No it's you pulling up in a pony old seventies saloon.

Speed/ Safety: 6
If the motor's less than thirty year's old, the homicidal driver's lead foot will get you there quicker than most, but you take life into your own hands.

Damage: 7
Relatively cheap fare is inevitably topped up by subsequent dry cleaning bill to remove drivers' eau de kebab.

Entertainment: 7
Stunt man driving techniques, Magic FM and talk of the five wives back home.

Stretch Limo

Wow Factor: 7
Depends on the car. Blacked out ministerial Mercedes with crest: yes. White caddy with boomerang and screaming girls out the sunroof: no.

Speed/ Safety: 7
Hold ups and embarrassment when car gets stuck negotiating tight corners. Driver likely to quit if you poke your arse out the window one more time.

Damage: 8
With the fare split between six or seven, it's cheaper than a piggy back ride in Botswana. Bacardi Breezers from the mini bar are extra.

Entertainment: 9
Singing Derek & Clive songs out the window. TMF on the box. One man Jacuzzi if you pay extra. Hed Kandi Ibiza Anthems CD comes as standard.

Mum's Volvo Estate

Wow Factor: 1
Instruct Mother to pull up twenty yards before or after the venue to avoid goodbye kiss and lecture on drugs in front of amused crowd.

Speed/ Safety: 10
Mirror, signal, manoeuvre. Hand brake, throttle, clutch. The safest ride of your life.

Damage: 7
Free at the point of consumption, but expect hidden costs in the form of ironing, gardening and car washing chores.

Entertainment: 5
The chance to bond with Mother to a soundtrack of Chris Rea while your pills start kicking in.

WARM-UP VENUES:

During daylight or the early evening, when the disco's doors are closed, many club species can be found socializing in alternative environments.

● Pub

Clientele: Workers, students, alcoholics

Distinguishing features:

1950s Mock Tudor   *Brass knick knacks*   *'Try our world famous homecooked Sunday roast'*

Soundtrack: Sky Sports, Who Wants To Be A Millionaire fruit machine

Most popular drink: Pint of lukewarm lager

● Gastropub

Clientele: Smug-looking couples

Distinguishing features:

1950s Mock Tudor, reconditioned with flowers   *Excessive quantity of people in square glasses*   *Overly elaborate menu description of fish'n'chips*

Soundtrack: Inoffensive jazz music, tedious chatter of variable rate index linked endowment policies

Most popular drink: Nice cold bottle of petit Chablis

ALTERNATIVE DRINKING PLACES

Though no substitute for the real thing, these licensed premises are useful places to recouperate, trade stories on how fucked they were last night and perform elaborate tricks with beer mats.

● Strip Club

Clientele: Short/fat/ugly businessmen, pavement shufflers in dirty macs

Distinguishing features:

  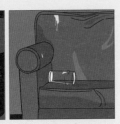

Neon-lit door guarded by gorilla *Footballers wives in dental floss.* *Wipe clean sofas.*

Soundtrack: Four to the floor Euro House and Ragga slow jams, clinking of pound coins in a pint glass.

Most popular drink: £15 glass of Virgin Cola

● Park Bench

Clientele: Tramps, teenagers, high strength cider connoisseurs

Distinguishing features:

Donated by the Women's Institute *Street murals* *Random low level violence*

Soundtrack: Incomprehensible mumbled threats, police sirens

Most popular drink: 1.5 litre bottle of White Lightning

DEVIL'S DANDRUFF

Can do the entire 'Hippy Hippy Shake' sequence from Cocktail move for move with his friend Matt

Testing straw – stopped using it as everyone thought he was trying to nick a bit of their drink for free

Optimistic weekly order of lychee and pomegranates yet to pay off

Tips received at a rate of never

Entire t-shirt collection is provided courtesy of brewery special offers

● Flamboyant Barman *Shakus Unappreciatea*

Shakus Unappreciatea has accumulated a wealth of drinks expertise via countless low-paid bar jobs across the world, and this predominantly Australian breed is always keen to impress with his knowledge and elaborate skills. Although more suited to an upscale New York hotel cocktail lounge, he is unfortunately stuck behind the bar in a grime-ridden nightclub where his customer's drink decisions are solely based upon how drunk it will get them and whether it's on special offer or not. While the clientele in both situations are often on the lookout for daring combinations of flavours and textures in this case that generally means trying to simultaneously neck two bottles of Chocolate Vodka Mudshake, a can of Red Bull and half a packet of pork scratchings rather than requesting an apple brandy sour with a twist of lime. However if anyone is brave enough to order a drink that doesn't come out of barrel or bottle, or merely ask for ice 'n' a slice in their Coke, they will be subjected to a fifteen minute display of spinning bottles, twirling mixers, straws flung behind ears and choreographed ice crushing, much to the annoyance of the backlogged queue of punters behind them. Expecting a Tom Cruise-style round of applause at the end of this heated display of virtuosity, *Shakus Unappreciatea* is often disappointed to be only met by a wet Boddingtons beer mat flung in his face and threats of physical violence from unserved customers.

Ways to alert your presence to barman

● SUCCESSFUL

✓ *Spend your whole time trying to make eye contact*
✓ *Avoid the main queue and sneak round the side by the till*
✓ *Become an attractive woman*

● UNSUCCESSFUL

✗ *Constantly wave a big wad of cash while shouting 'oi, oi!'*
✗ *Try to flick peanuts so they hit him on the nose*
✗ *Bang your fists up and down on the bar and sing 'Why Are We Waiting?'*

DISCO OUTFITS

Jackets

Shirts

Jackets

1. Playboy
2. Hustler
3. Readers Wives

Shirts

1. Just come from a titty bar, via Accounts
2. Just come from the estate, via Wetherspoons
3. Wishes he'd come from an estate, via public school

WHAT THEY SAY ABOUT YOU: MENSWEAR

Hats

 ①
 ②
 ③

① Reckons he's a bit tasty
② Reckons he's a bit arty
③ Reckons he's Guy Ritchie

Strides

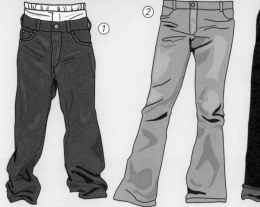

① Collects toy robots. Yet to discover belts
② First month at college. Yet to discover Topman
③ Aspiring Garage MC. Soon to discover HM Pleasure

Socks

① Predator
② Kindergarten Cop
③ Commando

Shoes

① I'm an individual
② I'm an individual
③ I'm an individual

DISCO OUTFITS

Jewellery

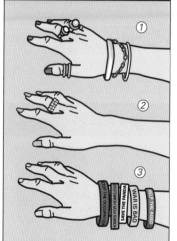

1. MTV Cribs
2. Bloomberg Dawn Traders
3. Hollyoaks

Hats

1. Never been out with anyone who doesn't have a highly paid job
2. Never been out with anyone who has a job
3. Never been out with anyone who's taken a bath

Skirts

  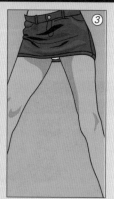

1. Dressed by John Lewis
2. Dressed by John Galliano
3. Dressed by John Leslie

WHAT THEY SAY ABOUT YOU: FEMALE FASHION

Shoes

① Love is respect, you'll have to earn it
② Love costs and i'm worth it
③ Chips cost, and i'm hungry

Tops

① Came to dance
② Came to be stared at
③ Came to be laughed at

Bags

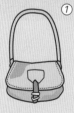  

① Bridget Jones
② Howard Jones
③ Indiana Jones

● Ticket Tout *Demandus Supplius*

The *Demandus Supplius* is a highly predatory breed that's commonly spotted congregated around the nearest public transport hub to potentially over-subscribed musical events. Using a distinctive mating cry of 'tickeeets, tickeeeets, buy and sell tickeets' it is continually on the search for a partner. Once found, the value of the tickets in question will fluctuate wildly depending on the other party's interest in buying or selling. If buying they will hear exotic talk of the evening's entertainment to come, the night in question suddenly becoming one of the most sought-after musical events of the century, even if it is just the Afro-Fusion side-project of the back-up keyboard player from *The Lion King*. Sellers on the other hand will be given a 'generous' offer of an old bus pass and a crumpled fiver to 'take them off their hands'. Although its wares are generally suitable only for loners or couples who enjoy sitting in two completely different parts of a venue the *Demandus Supplius* is an aggressive salesman whoever the target. Using everything from deceit ('Nah, it goes backwards at this one son - Row X is like practically being on stage'), anxiety ('you better hurry up, I promised them to this other bloke and he'll be back in a tick') and flattery ('tell you what I like your face so I'll let you buy them both') he is well versed in all forms of verbal trickery. However the emergence of the *Ebay Computerus* means this breed is potentially on the cusp of extinction and will soon have to resort to other, more traditional, forms of entrepreneurialism (plumbing scams, flogging hot stereos down the pub, homemade porno with the missus) in order to survive.

Related Species

● **Pirate DVD Salesman**
Best Selling Item: *Star Wars III (unique Asian subtitles and 'cinema crowd' effect version)*

● **Dodgy Cigarette Dealer**
Best Selling Item: *Marlboro Reds covered in Spanish health warnings*

● **Kerb Crawler Minicab**
Best Selling Item: *Sudden fare increase half way through journey*

DEVIL'S DANDRUFF

Bought a crateful of hooky Mamma Mia sweatshirts with his mate Dave. Sells them to Yank tourists for £25. Yours for a tenner

Terminator-style radar - can spot the bizzies from over 500 yards away

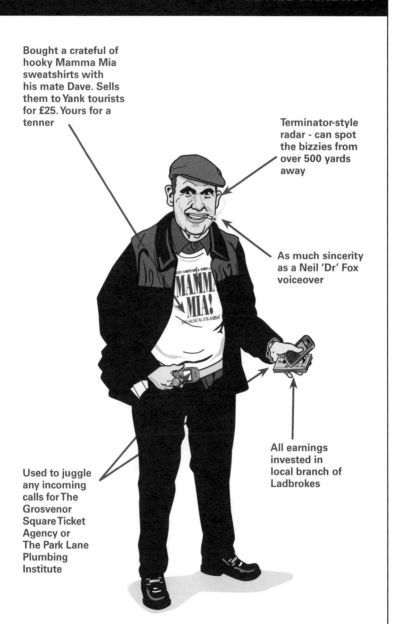

As much sincerity as a Neil 'Dr' Fox voiceover

All earnings invested in local branch of Ladbrokes

Used to juggle any incoming calls for The Grosvenor Square Ticket Agency or The Park Lane Plumbing Institute

● **Mobile Dealer** *Shiftus Peacockae*

It is a constant mystery how a minority of species in clubland maintain their luxurious lifestyles without ever holding down a job. The *Trustafarian* for instance, although an exceptionally dim-witted and lazy mammal, has a steady income stream because Daddy owns a network of sweatshops in Indonesia. The *Shiftus Peacockae* is another such example, ironically relying on the latter to uphold its standard of living. Travelling door to door, *Shiftus Peacockae* provides an essential service for middle class casual drug users who are too frightened to visit council estates or trust shadowy strangers in clubs. His fast, discreet, quality service feels less like an illicit transaction to his well heeled clientele, who would surely become prison 'bitches' if they were ever caught in the act. *Shiftus Peacockae*'s business set-up is ingenious. Customers phone their orders into a pirate garage station (popular among white professionals who 'wanna be down'). The radio deejay then relays the orders over the air in the guise of 'shout outs' to Mobile Dealer, who is listening in the Mercedes Jeep. Orders received, he speeds from Georgian terrace to loft conversion day and night, accumulating substantial monies as he goes. With life savings and liberty at stake, more sensible species would perhaps attempt to hide away their ill-gotten gains from public view. Not so Mobile Dealer, who is programmed by nature to splurge uncontrollably on blacked-out low riders, monogrammed manbags and impossibly sparkly rings; status symbols which tend to give the game away at the local DHSS, who are led to believe that a part time cashier's job at Woolworth's can support such finery.

SPEED DIAL NUMBERS:
1. 'FRIEND' IN COLUMBIA
2. 'FRIEND' AT THE
   PORT AUTHORITY
3. PAROLE OFFICER
4. SELFRIDGES MENSWEAR
5. SOLICITORS
   (NO WIN NO FEE)
6. DIAL-A-HONEY CHATLINE

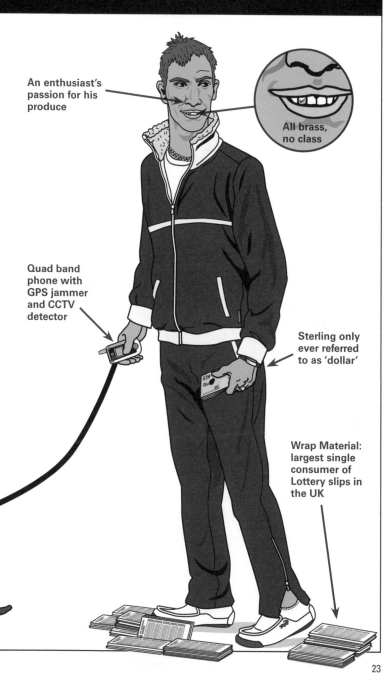

An enthusiast's passion for his produce

All brass, no class

Quad band phone with GPS jammer and CCTV detector

Sterling only ever referred to as 'dollar'

Wrap Material: largest single consumer of Lottery slips in the UK

● Bedroom DJ *Juvenae Masterbatum*

A close relative of Box Boy and extremely distant cousin of Superstar DJ, the bedroom variety is a brooding adolescent who shuns traditional paths of employment, personal development and dalliances with love in favour of the almighty deck, mixer and Faithless 12". Typically found in the bedroom furthest away from his parents in the family home (Dad isn't a big fan of early DJ Hell), this solitary species repeats an endless cycle of rituals at his home-made temple in the hope that one day he might, just might, become the new Brandon Block. This species often displays abnormal behavioural traits for a male in his late adolescence. While most healthy boys would have posters of Ferraris and Abi Titmuss on their walls, Bedroom DJ opts for promotional posters of expensive scratch needles and turntable equipment. Indeed, the same can be said for mix tapes; giving existing and prospective girlfriends two-hour journeys into Tribal House as opposed to the traditional Nick Drake/ Coldplay/ Brian Eno combo. Rarely spotted inside a club (unless it's to see a touring scratch champion), but can be identified by sun-starved skin, hairy palms and threadbare Nervous Records t-shirt.

Daily Routine

1. Rewire cartridges
2. Buff brass plack on limited edition Technics
3. Re-alphabetise records
4. Buff and re-alphabetise collection of pornography
5. Reread and memorise a chapter from 24hr Party People
6. Review scratch technique on digi camera
7. Record new tunes in log book
8. Watch girls walk to/from school out of window
9. Buff and re-alphabetise collection of pornography
10. Record continuous six-hour Trance mix (interrupted by toast and Marmite from Mum)

CLUB FLYERS EXPLAINED

The primary role of a flyer is to mislead the clubber into thinking he/ she will hear their favourite music in inspiring surroundings with attractive members of the opposite sex, while reaching a state of euphoria never achieved before. The reality is in fact decidedly different from the picture painted on flyers, but despite countless disappointing nights out on a promise from the promoter, punters are wooed back via sophisticated language and imagery, promising that something interesting might, just might happen if you come again.

52 MC's, 84 DJ's, 5 Arenas: the promoter has a lot of mates who want to be DJs and he has a problem saying no.

10pm 'till very late: the venue only has a pub license but the landlord will wing it until the bizzies arrive.

200w sound system: sounds impressive but actually isn't.

20K sound system: you will not be able to hear properly for the next five days.

Are You Ready For..?: hopefully the answer is yes, otherwise promoter has wasted a lot of time and money putting this night on.

Back To Back: two deejays who haven't got a full 2 hour set of records play together to make up the numbers.

Come With Peace And Love In Your Hearts: there is a major gun problem with the clientele.

Extended Set: the promoter is saving money and has bunged the DJ an extra fifty to play all night.

Exclusive Set: DJ can't get more than one gig per night.

Soundclash: different 'crews' play against each other, though they largely have the same records bought at HMV.

Legendary DJ: used to be really popular but got too old/ tired/ drug addled to cut it and faded into obscurity.

Ladies Free Before 11: club generally full of geezers.

Live PA: woman/man singing to backing track on makeshift stage of beer crates and MDF in 'Come Dancing'-style glittery outfit.

New School DJ: unheard-of DJ that was mates at school of the promoter, or the box boy of a bigger deejay name on the flyer.

No Jeans or Trainers: the venue is downmarket but wishes to be perceived as upmarket.

No Suits: the venue is upmarket but wishes to be perceived as downmarket.

Old School Reunion: see legendary DJs.

Original and the best: a rival promoter has nicked the same idea for the night and is doing a better job of it.

Pay in Advance/More on the Door: the promoter needs to pay his leccy bill before the gig happens.

Picture of sexy girl: the chances of this or any similar looking woman appearing is virtually nil, but you should come just in case.

Picture of beautiful people drinking champagne: full of suits on expense accounts.

Picture of euphoric dance scene: this might happen if the DJ plays to the crowd, not his four Belgian Techno mates in the DJ booth.

Plus Guests/and Friends: see 'New School DJ'.

Psychedelic graphics: this is an illegal rave in an old post office organised by travellers.

ROAR: the bouncers are snobs/ racists/ Nazis and prefer not to let anyone in at all.

Sophisticated Crowd: bottled beer five times normal price.

● Flyer Designer *Nocturni Graftus*

Behold, the rarest sighted species of them all. *Nocturni Graftus* is a solitary recluse that, like his distant cousin the Club Journalist, shapes the identity of clubland without ever setting one Converse clad foot on a dancefloor. The bright lights, aggressive behaviour and poor choice of cider brands to be found at the club are all alien to Flyer Designer. In fact, *Graftus'* entire body of flyer artwork is based on his two lone disco experiences, being the Clacton High Summer School Disco of 1987 and the saucy lesbian dancing scene off Basic Instinct. Living a hermit-like existence the house is only left when important supplies (milk, bread, coffee, Dairylea Cheese Slices) run out. As a result Flyer Designer has very little contact with the opposite sex. References to women in his flyers originate from the Next Directory lingerie section, and although not unattractive, the closest he comes to the real thing is unfortunately the vacuum packed used panties that Japanese flyer collectors trade in return for rare artwork.

Every meal a banquet

Mac Graveyard: emotional attachment to defunct gear akin to that of a small furry pet

DEVIL'S DANDRUFF

Permanent facet lock and tick in neck similar to that of a caged animal

Obligatory limited edition overpriced Japanese toy

i-Tunes pumps out Kruder & Dorfmeister on heavy rotation

DEVIL'S DANDRUFF

● Shop DJ *Juvenae Narcissisus*

To be found playing breakbeat party classics in a youth-orientated high-street chainstore, Shop DJ (and posse of boy band lookalike mates) is the embodiment of club culture gone overground. A variety of male peacock, he is resplendent in ostentatious midprice designer sports brands and a willing ambassador of metrosexual personal grooming regimes. His meticulously planned sets are somewhat hampered by head-office requirements to announce this week's offers ('half price on selected hair care products and three for two on baggy fit t-shirts') every 20 minutes. Currently boning the assistant manager at lunch in the store cupboard, he commonly provides an entry level shag into the nightclub industry for wide-eyed teenage girls on a spending spree up town from the 'burbs. Once had the store evacuated after introducing his own strobe and smoke machine (only £39.99 from Maplin) in the mistaken belief that it would 'race things up a little'. Shop DJ aspires to progress from his late night Thursday clothes store gig to a Saturday afternoon department store slot where he's more likely to be spotted by Judge Jules, on the browse for directional wristbands or a new toaster.

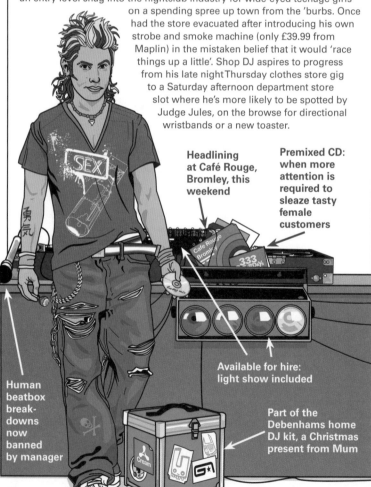

Headlining at Café Rouge, Bromley, this weekend

Premixed CD: when more attention is required to sleaze tasty female customers

Human beatbox break-downs now banned by manager

Available for hire: light show included

Part of the Debenhams home DJ kit, a Christmas present from Mum

● Postcode Plonker *Persona Deficienae*

The right side of trendy: anything too outlandish is frowned upon at work →

Just like Jamie Oliver →

Debating whether it's still cool to get a Japanese tattoo ↑

Still can't get the shoes right →

Healthy in bank balance but lacking in personality, Postcode Plonker is under the mistaken impression that if moving to an area that was once (before the property developers squeezed all the life out) a happening, edgy place, then he too will become a happening, edgy individual. Pouring over estate agents' brochures (all featuring photos of an out-of-focus woman on a designer sofa, a bloke on a running machine and a building of historic interest that is no doubt soon to be pulled down by aforementioned developers), he settles on a ludicrously overpriced 'loft style' flat made of MDF and corrugated iron, located above an £8-a-pop gastro-kebab house. Then immediately complains to the council about the noise. Swiftly moving into his new persona, Postcode Plonker will appropriate exactly the same style, haircut and possessions as his fellow inhabitants in a bid to display a new, hard-won individuality. A well-paid, but ultimately pointless job, as well as strong paternal financial assistance, enables this creature to spend evenings in upmarket clubs and bars, costly cappuccino or bottled beer in hand, regaling females with details of the short proximity to his current abode. Despite the rising costs of transport, there are few takers for the offer of late-night hospitality, and Postcode Plonker spends most evenings on the brief walk home alone.

Pointless Clubbing Accessories

Nightclubs offer many one of the few chances in the week to be more experimental with their appearance. However while most utilise this opportunity wisely there is a species whose primary concern is in attracting as much personal attention as possible. For this breed the most potent weapon at their disposal is the procurement of a seemingly pointless accessory.

FAIRY WINGS

Wow Factor: 1
Matched only in the impact stakes by oversized dungarees, pork pie hats and Star Trek novelty ties.

Ease: 5
Can only really be worn in conjunction with a pink tutu or bridesmaid dress. Accompanying wand is cumbersome on the dancefloor.

Pointlessness: 10
Unless you attach some sort of motor to them, they don't make you fly. Likely to repel 99.9% of population.

Fun Factor: 8
Wearers are commonly so full of childlike joy and wonderment there could be a cataclysmic earthquake on the dancefloor and they'd still be smiling.

WHISTLE

Wow Factor: 1
Keen-eyed clubbers who fear for their hearing will spot the whistle a mile off and move straight to the opposite end of the disco.

Ease: 3
Few skills required. Will come even more naturally if you have a part time job as a P.E. teacher, dinner lady or New York traffic cop.

Pointlessness: 5
Deafening those around you, throwing the DJ off his job with out-of-time whistling, spraying the dancefloor with gob. The negatives outweigh the positives.

Fun Factor: 8
You can respond loudest when the DJ cries 'Let me hear some noise!'. Bonus points also include the ability to drunkenly direct traffic at busy junctions after closing time.

DEVIL'S TRUMP

DEVIL'S TRUMPS

GIMP

Wow Factor: 10
Bystanders' minds will be filled with a confusing combination of amazement and disgust.

Ease: 2
Will have to come in contact with a lot of weirdos to find one suitable. Also double price entry on the door.

Pointlessness: 2
Despite initial air of superficiality actually is quite useful: can order gimp to clean shoes, start fights and stand in the bar queue for you.

Fun Factor: 3
The novelty of having to change the shitted pants of a middle-aged man with social problems soon wears off.

DOG IN A BAG

Wow Factor: 9
It's a cute little dog! In a bag! In a club! Only to be beaten when someone brings a penguin in a top hat along.

Ease: 2
Alongside finding a bag both suitably dinky and robust, dog will require a constant supply of Pedigree Chum and small plastic bones that squeak.

Pointlessness: 10
Exclusively practised by neurotic women desperate for attention, or extreme sexual deviants trying to get one up on the Richard Gere hamster myths.

Fun Factor: 3
Great until the dog starts getting the runs and crapping everywhere or begins howling during a breakdown.

SUNGLASSES AT NIGHT

Wow Factor: 6
Onlookers instantly think (a) you've had a fight and lost (b) cut-price corrective plastic surgery didn't work out so well (c) prick.

Ease: 1
Simple. However you can't tell if the person dancing next to you is interested, attractive or even the right sex. Drunken idiots try them on without asking all night.

Pointlessness: 7
By wearing them you are showing your disdain for normal social conventions and contempt for 'the rules'. However this air of cool is shattered every time you walk into a door or bump into a stool.

Fun Factor: 6
Slim chance that people will think you're an international playboy/ girl and want to hang off your arm all night. Emphasis on the word slim.

DEVIL'S TRUMPS

DEVIL'S DANDRUFF

Descriptions and terminologies found within club listings are mind numbingly confusing affairs. Club journalists are commonly frustrated creative writers, conjuring up their own dialect at the click of a mouse and expecting everyone else to understand what they're babbling on about. The majority are also too long in the tooth to venture out of the house after 11pm (especially if there's an Inspector Morse repeat on), so half of the information is made up. These factors combine to make the average club listing a confusing flight of fancy that rarely bears any relation to the quality of event in hand.

● **Beefed up soundsystem:**
Technical specification of speakers printed on press release.

● **Decks'n'FX:**
There will be a lot of whooshing noises over every other tune.

● **Dress to impress:**
The Guestlist girl thinks she's in a Studio Line advert, and wants everyone to look the same.

● **Discerning crowd:**
Full of late thirty something couples who now rarely go clubbing as it's so difficult to find a decent baby-sitter.

● **Eclectic mash-up:**
The DJ can't beat mix very well but will give it a go anyway.

● **Edgy location:**
Leave your valuables at home.

● **Exploring the roots:**
The DJ will play some Roy Ayres/ James Brown at some point.

● **Featuring the new breed:**
Same as the old breed, only younger and cheaper.

● **Featuring upfront tunez:**
Tunes no one has/wants to hear of and will not dance to.

● **Full of attitude:**
Everyone looks at you like you're a cunt.

● **Glamourous location:**
They do Mai Tai's at the bar and there's a bloke in the bogs with some CK One and Chupa Chups.

● **Grungy vibe:**
The venue is a shit hole, wipe your feet as you leave.

● **It's 'four to the floor' all the way:**
More exciting term for generic Top 10 House.

● **Heavyweight line-up:**
DJs the writer has heard of.

● **Last one was a mash up:**
The promoter took the writer out to lunch last week.

● **Last one was a ram jam mash up:**
The promoter took the writer out to lunch last week and got him drunk.

● **Leftfield party:**
The girls look like blokes and the blokes have angular haircuts.

● **Legendary night:**
Writer remembers that night was vaguely fashionable for about a month three years ago.

● **Long running institution:**
Stopped being any good years ago but the promoter needs the money.

● **Low key venue:**
The tumbleweeds outnumber the punters.

CLUB LISTINGS EXPLAINED

● **Polysexual grooves:**
High possibility of seeing someone getting bummed in the corner.

● **Popular with bassheads:**
Full of geezers in baseball hats nodding a lot.

● **Professional mixologists:**
Allow 30 mins to get served a drink.

● **Resident big name DJ:**
Big name DJ may actually turn up if there's nothing better on offer.

● **Roadblock:** *The bouncers are nazis and make everyone queue, even though it's empty inside.*

● **Secret location:**
Promoter still desperately trying to find a venue after last one fell through.

● **Spread over three rooms:**
You will spend most of the evening wandering around like a lost sheep.

● **Street food:**
Bar serving warm Phileas Fogg crisps covered in sprayable cheese for £4 a pop.

● **Take no prisoners DJ style:**
Six hours of engine piston sounds and feedback.

● **Taking it back to where it all started:**
DJ not bought any new records since 1996.

● **The promoters have pulled out all the stops:**
Promoter has bought a slide projector and some balloons.

● **This is going to be a big one:**
Writer saw some flyposters for it on his way to work.

● **Tonight's essential party:**
There's nothing else on.

● **Truly diverse crowd:**
A couple of asian girls and a japanese bloke were spotted at the bar last time.

● **Twisted beats:**
You will not be able to whistle any of the records played.

● **Up for it crowd:**
There are loads of dealers there and the pills sometimes work.

● **Warehouse-style party:**
The only toilet in the venue will be backed up and overflowing within half an hour.

● **Weekend party people:**
Crowd spending half their week's wage on as much overpriced beer and pills as they can cram down their gobs in a bid to forget their hum-drum nine-to-five lives.

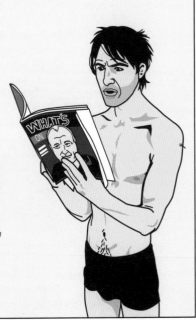

PART 2: ARRIVING

DEVIL'S DANDRUFF

Alarm clock face: would get you out of bed pretty sharpish if you woke up next to it

Style icon: the KGB officer in From Russia With Love

Doubles as match strike - even safety matches

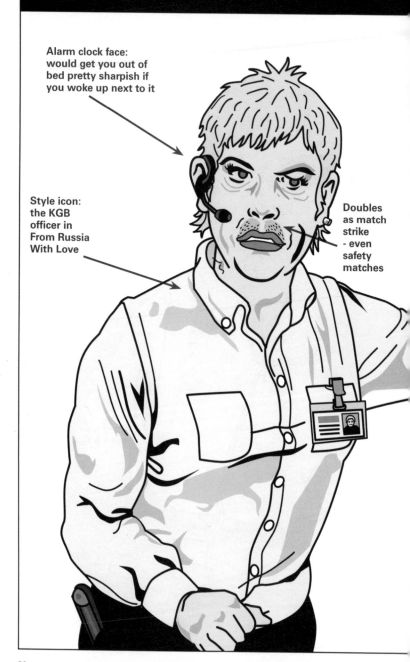

● Female Bouncer *Brutus Femmohomo*

Sporting a face that looks like it has spent the day sucking three month old lemons, Female Bouncer was unlikely to become a super-model. Many female species would employ extra personality and charm to offset poor looks, but *Brutus Femmohomo* supplements her unfortunate physicality with a level of charisma and empathy equalled only by that of an automated call-waiting system. *Brutus Femmohomo* developed formidable interpersonal skills during her previous incarnation as a traffic warden, learning that the best way to deal with public requests, however innocent or reasonable, is to completely ignore them. When interaction is required, it comes solely from a Robocop-style list of five choice phrases (see below) - few have ever heard her utter anything else. In spite of her diminutive size, she is the most feared bouncer of them all, so much so that even the other door security, all 20-stone bruisers themselves, are scared of her. Leaving the second her shift is over, little is known about her personal life, despite much after-hours speculation from the remaining club staff.

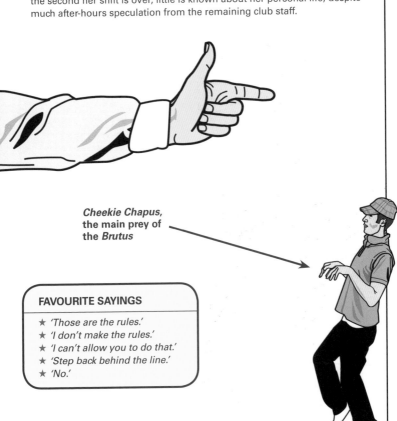

Cheekie Chapus, the main prey of the *Brutus*

FAVOURITE SAYINGS

★ 'Those are the rules.'
★ 'I don't make the rules.'
★ 'I can't allow you to do that.'
★ 'Step back behind the line.'
★ 'No.'

DEVIL'S DANDRUFF

● **Office Bloke** *Suitus*

No Jacket Required

Cologne: a blend of Davidoff and chicken tikka sandwich

Expression of individuality

Required reading in the boardroom

Although rare, it is occasionally possible to see *Suitus* venture away from his natural habitat (Pitcher & Piano, All Bar One, Wetherspoon's Wednesday Night Curry Club) to the unfamiliar surroundings of the subterranean nightclub. Celebrating the closure of a 'Big Deal' office bloke uses the occasion to impress colleagues/office totty with his deep understanding of dance culture, which in reality amounts to one CD (Leftism by Leftfield, bought because it showed off his new stereo nicely) and an article on Norman Cook in the Daily Express. With nothing more lining his stomach than a grabsize bag of Brannigans and five Flaming Ferrari cocktails, he breaks all codes of dress and conduct at the door, only gaining entry via a top-pocket bonus to the bouncer. Waiting at the bar for the DJ to play his request (Hot Chocolate's *You Sexy Thing*), Office Bloke will quickly give up on dancing, and get on with the serious business of ordering barrel loads of Orange Bacardi Breezer and slowly groping lone females' backsides. Such behaviour usually results in forced ejection from the premises, and the evening's frivolities end alone, drunkenly arguing with tramps, haggling with minicab drivers and throwing up over his shoes.

● The Venue Owner *Fatus Muntus*

Extremely frightening, fleshy species of unknown ethnic origin. Despite poor physical and mental capabilities, the Venue Owner dominates all in clubland's food chain. Barring ostentatious sports car, the grubby appearance belies obscene wealth accrued from various shady deals. Little or no appreciation of music, fashion or any culture beyond the accumulation of monies. Easily identified by distinctive aroma of stale beer, disinfectant and used £20 notes. Commonly found hovering around bar, eyeing lowly staff at cash till.

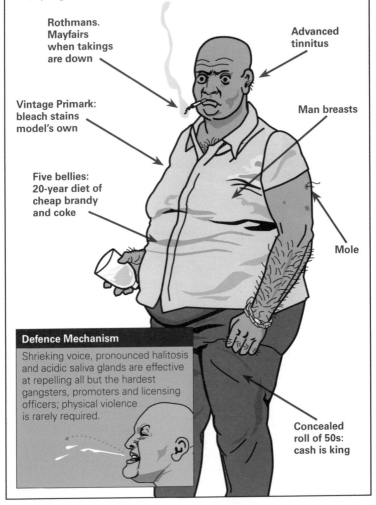

Rothmans. Mayfairs when takings are down

Advanced tinnitus

Vintage Primark: bleach stains model's own

Man breasts

Five bellies: 20-year diet of cheap brandy and coke

Mole

Defence Mechanism

Shrieking voice, pronounced halitosis and acidic saliva glands are effective at repelling all but the hardest gangsters, promoters and licensing officers; physical violence is rarely required.

Concealed roll of 50s: cash is king

DEVIL'S DANDRUFF

The only words she will utter with any sincerity all night are 'you're not going to get in'

In danger of developing repetitive strain injury due to habit of shaking head at majority of punters all evening

Has perfected clipboard 'poker' hold preventing any surreptitious snooping of guestlist names

Can withstand temperatures that would impress Captain Robert Scott

● Guestlist Girl *Clipboarus Holdus*

Standing on the door of a club, exposed to the elements (wind/rain/blaggers/minicab touts/geezers shouting 'Tits Out For The Lads' as they drive by) would to most be an idea of hell. Not so for Guestlist Girl, a breed whose natural state is at the head bouncer's side, with clip board in one hand and a Vodka Lime Soda in the other; the negatives of the role being greatly outweighed by the unimaginable power she is afforded. Strutting slowly up and down the queue, quantifying the crowd's sartorial hits and misses, Guestlist Girl spends less time performing her primary function (letting important people in for free) than as self-elected arbiter of taste for the club, handing out tough love to punters with a string of damning one liners ('Be honest, would you let yourself in?') and killer stares of disapproval. When important people on the list do turn up and demand her attention, Guestlist Girl's demeanour flicks from vicious Rottweiler to cuddly Chihuahua. Ever hopeful of landing the MTV weekday morning presenter's role, she performs the role of hostess with immaculate perfection, an efficient pole-greaser when the situation requires. This position requires a high level of expenditure on flouncy Marc Jacobs tops, which are beyond the means of her basic wage. It is necessary therefore to operate a multitude of fraudulent scams under the promoter's nose which would make the Kray twins look like small time pussycats.

Top Scams

● *No 1:* Going to the back of the queue, taking bribes to let them in for free, claiming ignorance of the whole thing when they finally get to the door.

● *No 2:* Selling pills to punters in the queue, then getting the bouncer to confiscate them later.

● *No 3:* Confiscating clothes/accessories according to a ficticious dress code and flogging them on ebay the next day.

● **Blagger** *Cheekie Chapus*

At first glance many mistake the *Cheekie Chapus* for its almost identical cousin - the *Twatus Maximus*. While both look very similar - usually adorned in the same distinctive markings of British casual labels - the temperament of the *Cheekie Chapus* is somewhat different. A more nimble mammal, it prefers the art of opportunity over that of aggression. Intoxicants are rarely paid for, as not only does the mammal spend the entire evening poncing smokes off punters, it is also highly skilled at stealing drinks when the barman's back is turned. If money is needed it is often provided through the selling of paracetamol or bags of sugar to gullible first-year degree students. Spends majority of the night looking for an opportune moment to lift the DJ's record box.

Top Three Door Blags

● *No 1:* **The Distraction**
Showing bouncer stolen mobiles inside jacket or pointing in the distance while mates sneak in behind his back.

● *No 2:* **The Fire Exit**
Pays full entry price, and proceeds straight to the fire exit ... friends in free, strangers at half price.

● *No 3:* **The Bum Rush**
Gathering of posse and running screaming *en masse* at the door and steaming through.

DEVIL'S DANDRUFF

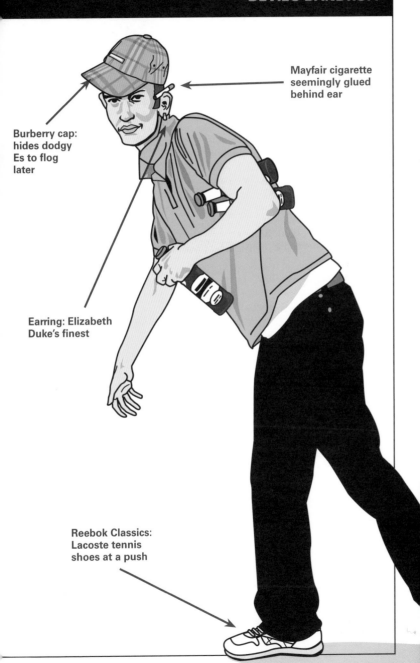

Mayfair cigarette seemingly glued behind ear

Burberry cap: hides dodgy Es to flog later

Earring: Elizabeth Duke's finest

Reebok Classics: Lacoste tennis shoes at a push

DEVIL'S DANDRUFF

Disco Contraband:
Ingenious methods of stashing the goods

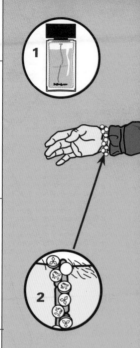

● *No 1:* **Makeshift alcohol atomiser:**
Fill an old aftershave bottle with
booze and spray away.

Pros: Undetectable by security. Easy to stash. Good ice-breaker: 'Can I spray something naughty in your mouth?'

Cons: Bottle must be fancy - Father's ancient Kouros won't impress. Aftershave residue tastes like battery acid.

● *No 2:* **Disco biscuit bracelet:**
Elasticised e-chain.

Pros: Easily nibbled at wearer's discretion. Directional fashion in a 1980s pop-sock kind of way. Doubles as Chinese love beads.

Cons: Looks a bit too feminine on blokes. Liable to melt on contact with wrist sweat. Needs lots of jimmys to look authentic.

● *No 3:* **Pac-a-sac:**
Colostomy bag, liquor and a straw.

Pros: Discreet straw means you can sip all night long. Cocktails are well shaken by the first dance. Look like you're packing more heat in the trouser department (boys only).

Cons: Body-temp booze tastes yuk. If the bag bursts you're in trouble, especially with light grey trousers. Usually only secondhand bags available, which is just wrong.

● *No 4:* **Bolivian dandruff:**
Pour coke/speed on to shoulders.

Pros: No fiddly wraps, which always split in any case. Girls/boys permanently on your arm looking for love bites. Possibly mistaken for trendy/ironic glitter gel.

Cons: One gust of wind and it's all gone Pete Tong. Onlookers mistake you for a soap dodger. Crook neck from repeated turning of head to sniff.

DISCO CONTRABAND

DEVIL'S DANDRUFF

● Licensing Officer *Accreditus Sinistae*

Eyes: can count how many people are in a room in seconds

Watch: accurate to 1/1000th of a second yet always seems to be five minutes faster than everyone else's

Pockets: can store keys, mobile and at least three A6 envelopes stuffed full of cash

Shoes: for kicking dodgy electrical wiring

This creature's meek appearance may suggest otherwise, but Licensing Officer is without doubt one of the most powerful beasts in clubland. Armed with nothing more than a clipboard, Maglite torch and an alarmingly anal respect for 'correct procedure', he has the power to shut down entire venues with a flick of his ballpoint. His appearance will turn the most hard nosed venue owner into a subservient sycophant as they give him a royal tour of the venue, all the while hoping that Promoter is swiftly kicking the underage kids and dealers out the back (*Fig 1*). Often carries out surprise inspections in response to complaints made by 'members of the public', who seem to be remarkably well-informed on licensing procedure and strangely share concerns that would only really be of interest if they owned a rival club two doors down. In the event of any serious problems (*Figs 2,3* and *4*), Venue Owner will ask *Accreditus Sinistae* to look after their wallet while they go and sort them out. Frequent visits commonly result in the Officer being offered the job, in a spirit of community well-being, to dispose of the big bag of drugs confiscated by the bouncers (*Fig 5*).

Fig 1

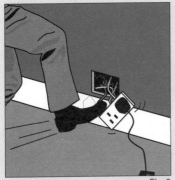

Fig 2

Fig 3

Fig 4

Fig 5

DEVIL'S DANDRUFF

● **What to say:**
'Hi. I'm in town promoting a great new stage play I'm in and I'd really like to "have the time of my life" in your fine establishment this evening.'

● **What to say:**
'Heya babe. Yeah, it's me Lisa l'Anson. You know, I'm well famous and I do everything - stand in for Vanessa Feltz on the radio, tampon ad voiceovers, the lot - so let me in, yeah?'

● Pretend to be someone famous

Method: Using a photocopier, enlarge one of the faces opposite and attach to your face with a piece of string. Potential to look a bit pony is high, so use only at clubs with shortsighted doormen and/or bad lighting systems. For increased levels of success try and get a mate with a decent camera (not a disposable) to shout 'over here' at you a lot.

Pros:

✓ Free Breezers all night.
✓ Everybody wants to have/make your babies.
✓ They put a little red rope around your table.

Cons:

✗ Black & white laser copies don't really cut it.
✗ Hard to convince doormen that a major Hollywood star would be wearing a battered pair of Reebok Classics.

● Bouncer *Gorillus Horribilus*

Seldom is a breed in clubland so specifically evolved for a sole purpose than that of *Gorillus Horribilus*; the purpose being the placing of a 16 stone inanimate piece of meat between the queue and the cash till. As far as he is concerned however, the job of Security Guard (the preferred title) is one of charming host to the ladies and subtle diplomacy to quarrelsome gents, executed with the benefit of fifteen years in 'The Force', ten years of bare knuckle fighting, and five years of spit and sawdust prostitution since the wife 'fucked off with some queer'. With hours of downtime on the job, *Gorillus Horribilus* has evolved an incredible mastery of conversational technique, usually of the long drawn out, opinionated variety. Having no life experience beyond standing in doors and fighting is no barrier to dispensing pearls of wisdom to beleaguered co-workers on everything from index-linked endowments to the finer points of Thatcher's Conservative manifesto of '85. Despite listening to thousands of hours of dance music, *Gorillus Horribilus* cannot distinguish between trance, hip hop or any other household genre, preferring instead to hum Chris Rea ditties while dealing with the great unwashed. When prospective punters enquire about music policy, he points solemnly to a sign above his work post: 'Do not ask stupid questions, as a smack in the mouth often offends'.

FAVOURITE SAYINGS

★ *'I aint the shit on no one's shoes'*
★ *'You're a big man, but you're in bad shape. With me it's a full time job. Now behave yourself'*
★ *'Don't play with the bull son, you'll get the horns'*
★ *'Extra chilli sauce on that please love'*

Tools of the Trade

● **Huge Torch:** For shining in the eyes and jamming in the kidneys.

● **Beta Blockers:** For when the 'roid rage kicks in.

● **Effey's Kebab Meal Deal:** Twice a night. Three if it's slow at the club.

DEVIL'S DANDRUFF

Claims battle scars are souvenirs from the Falklands. Actually incurred during rows with violent bodybuilder girlfriend

Only show emotion during *Match Of The Day*

For show only: venue owner too tight to splash out on a radio system that actually works

Knuckle Scabs: resulting from baboon style posture

DEVIL'S DANDRUFF

● The Empty Record Box

Method: Rock up to the club carrying what looks like a very heavy record box (school drama training needed here). Claim you are (or are with) the DJ. Headphones round the neck will help add an extra level of gravitas. Always good to act a bit harassed 'hurry up - I'm meant to be on in five minutes'.

Success rating: 9
Potential beating behind the dustbins ratio if found out: 7
Embarrassment if escorted to the decks and asked to play: 10

Pros:
✓ Likely to get all your mates in too.
✓ Can also use the DJ booth as a free cloakroom.
✓ Chance to get 'Strings Of Life' signed by the DJ.

Cons:
✗ Lugging a big record box about, which, empty or not, is a pain in the arse.
✗ May develop status anxiety over the number of stickers on box compared to the real DJs.
✗ Drunken hens will approach and ask you to play Kylie or do a birthday shout out.

Advanced Blagging

● Have a mix CD to hand if you do actually have to start playing.

● Return to the door and arrange an extra few names on the list.

● Demand your fee in cash before setting foot in the DJ booth. Then leg it.

DEVIL'S DANDRUFF

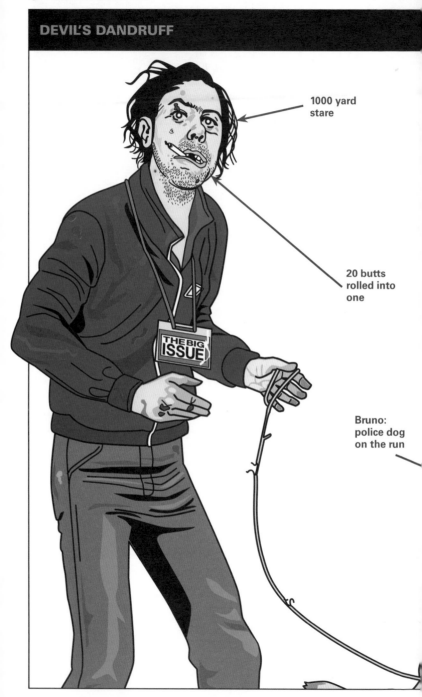

1000 yard stare

20 butts rolled into one

Bruno: police dog on the run

● Beggar & Dog *Muntus & Muttus*

This dishevelled species hails from a local working class dynasty that spans several centuries, but due to doorstep regeneration, Beggar's indigenous habitat has transformed into a confusing melee of upper-mid-range restaurants selling salt-crusted cod on a bed of Puy lentils and bustling nightclubs full of asexual youths dressed in 21st-century clown outfits. His revenge on the uninvited march of gentrification is to scare well-to-do punters in line at the door queue using three dynamic techniques. (1) The drunken shouting of class war rhetoric and laughing loudly at clubbers' 'challenging' outfits. (2) Joining the queue and casually groping unsuspecting women. (3) The abandonment of basic personal hygiene rules, combined with hourly consumption of Kestrel Super and a flea-ridden German Shepherd to create a lingering acrid stench. All the above send sensitive clubbers running to rival bars for refuge, much to the annoyance of Promoter. At the first sign of the Police however, Beggar will scuttle off home, to resume his normal life as senior careers officer at the local Job Centre.

Ador, the brand with *four* stripes

Preferred Refreshment

● **No 1:**
White Ace: 7.5%
Sharp, refreshing taste cuts through the kebab meat. And the intestines.

● **No 2:**
Drakkar Noir: 80%
From the back of the bathroom cabinet.

● **No 3:**
All-Purpose Brush Cleaner: 110%
Easily procured from neighbour's lock up. One way ticket to mogadon.

DEVIL'S DANDRUFF

● Create A Diversion

Method: Orchestrate a disturbance with your mates to distract the door staff - the more elaborate the blag, the greater satisfaction achieved when successful. Most effective is the drugs overdose: one of your mates collapses outside the door in a fit; you scream at the bouncers that he just bought a pill inside the club. While staff rush to prevent a death on their doorstep, you and your mates steam the door.

Success rating: 6
Chances of feeling guilty after the blag: 10
Chances of being banned for life by venue if rumbled: 10

Pros

✓ Enjoy seeing the look of fear on the bouncers' faces.
✓ You get to lecture Venue Owner of the dangers of drugs.
✓ Get paid in beer by the management to keep quiet.

Cons

✗ Not so good for the fit faker, who spends a night looking sheepish in A&E.
✗ Fit faker looks like a plum if the bouncers don't buy it.
✗ Done often enough, bouncers may get wise and end up ignoring real overdoses.

Other Bouncer Diversions

● Release brakes on nearby hotdog wagon and send it crashing into queue.

● Slip a tramp a couple of quid to constantly demand that he be let in to see his mate Johnny.

● Set up a nearby stall selling cut price MA1 jackets, steroids and cattle prods.

DEVIL'S DANDRUFF

● Underage Clubber *Immaturum Pubescae*

Obsessed with a burning desire to stand in long door queues, loiter round the DJ booth, suck on fluorescent alcopops and stare in wonder at fully mature females/males, the underage clubber is regularly sighted performing the rites of passage of a juvenile in advanced puberty at the nightclub. Eager to establish a level of maturity beyond his/her means, this resourceful breed employs a number of deceptive tactics to ensure acceptance into adult disco life. Elaborate ID, loud talk of mortgages and mum's old costume jewellery squeezed onto wedding fingers are favourites here. The female of the species (always a winner with married thirtysomething males) is infinitely more successful in this pursuit, with the males (chainsmoking Aled Jones look-alikes with acne) usually being sent home for an early bath.

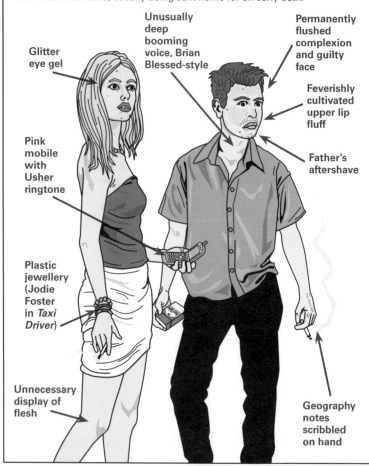

Glitter eye gel

Unusually deep booming voice, Brian Blessed-style

Permanently flushed complexion and guilty face

Feverishly cultivated upper lip fluff

Father's aftershave

Pink mobile with Usher ringtone

Plastic jewellery (Jodie Foster in *Taxi Driver*)

Unnecessary display of flesh

Geography notes scribbled on hand

Make Your Own Fake ID

The majority of fake ID cards are appallingly obvious, featuring the owner's date of birth in suspiciously large letters, dubious sounding organisations and bits of hair caught under the plastic laminate. Despite this however most money-hungry landlords and venue owners turn a blind eye - as long as you've made an effort then they're in less trouble if the bizzies raid the joint.

With that in mind here are a number of cards that can be easily cut out for your own use. For an extra air of authenticity it can be worth lightly coating the lid of a bottle of aspirin with ink and using that as an official-looking stamp over the photo.

POLISH DRIVING LICENCE Kørekort.

Nøm: ....

Dat I Birth: / /

POLSKA
GDAŃSK

Is Nø:POL 47876432-1234

Is allow to driving a ~~three~~/four wheeled car throughout Poland

Signo: ....

SUPAFILM Video Club

Name: _____

Date Of Birth: _____

Membership No: _____

Allowed to rent:

PG 12 15 18 XXX

DEVIL'S DANDRUFF

● On the List (Straight Style)

Method: Claim you are on the guest list. When they cannot find you come up with some kind of excuse as to why you were supposed to be on the list. You're a friend of the promoter. The DJ put you down. Your mate cleans the toilets. You clean the toilets. Anything. Depending on the popularity of the club and the patience of the guestlist-holder there is a slight possibility that, if they really can't put up with your non-stop arguing/bullshit, they may just let you in. Seems to work a lot better for Eddie Murphy than anyone else.

Success rating: 8
Level of respect from fellow punters if failure: Low

Pros:

✓ Very straightforward.

Cons:

✗ Once unsuccessful you are a marked man - difficult to try any other moves as bouncers will be looking out for you.
✗ Very much reliant on the individual's own levels of charisma, debate and bullshit.
✗ You may be made to clean the toilets.

DOOR BLAGS

● On the List (Sneaky Style)

Method: Claim you are on the guest list but you don't know what name you've been put under. Give some nonsensical moniker such as 'Smokin' Jo'. The more ludicrous the better. While this name is being looked for try and read one of the other names that is actually on the list. Then suggest this one, that it is your normal name, or better yet your mate's name.

Success rating: 7
Potential that 'Smokin' Jo' is actually on the list: Low

Pros:
✓ A good tidy routine.
✓ Can help you get mates in too.

Cons:
✗ Sometimes list is too well hidden.
✗ You have to make sure you don't choose the name of anyone personally known to the guestlist holder.
✗ You have to be good at reading upside down.

DEVIL'S DANDRUFF

A reliable method of procuring free entry on the door is to pose as someone of importance. And one of the best ways to appear important is with a business card. For effective use, the cards must be accompanied by authentic patter.

No. 1 Drinks Company PR

Ouzoade

Alix Smith
Marketing Manager
The Ouzoade Company

Enterprise House
259 Scruton Road
London
EC2A 4GHT

T:020 077 2279   M:07916 74532   E:alixs@ouzoade.com

The story:
You're looking for a venue to spend next month's marketing budget, giving away free bottles of your latest Ouzo and Lemonade alcopop. This club is on the shortlist.

Success rating:
High. Drinks companies are so huge they normally have a number of different PR companies working for them. Even if the guestlist holder is up to speed on the outsourcing ventures of multinational distilleries, you can still wing it.

Perks:
Likely to be introduced to the bar manager – high possibility of free drinks all night too.

Optional props:
Garish designer clothes worn badly.

THE BUSINESS CARD BLAG

Cut out the following tried and tested designs and paste on to a good quality card or design your own. Then memorise the following stories, and you should avoid queues and charges hence forth.

No. 2 TV Researcher

Productions Limited

Alix Smith
Researcher

Chat Behind
Enterprise House
259 Scruton Road
London
EC2A 4GHT

T:020 077 2279
M:07916 74532

a.smith@chatbehind.com
www.chatbehind.com

The story:
You are researching a massive new TV show and you're looking for potential venues to film in/punters to star in.

Success rating: Moderate – previously a sure-fire blag, the allure of working in television has waned somewhat over the past couple of years. Guestlist holder may suspect you are filming the next series of Hitman & Her.

Perks:
Few. They are unlikely to let a big posse in with you, nor look after you once inside.

Optional props:
Clothes worn too young for your age. Clipboard with other venues listed.

DEVIL'S DANDRUFF

A reliable method of procuring free entry on the door is to pose as someone of importance. And one of the best ways to appear important is with a business card. For effective use, the cards must be accompanied by authentic patter.

No. 3 Licensing Officer

Alix Smith
Council Licensing Officer

Tower Hamlicks Council
Enterprise House
259 Scruton Road
London
EC2A 4GHT

tel: 020 077 2279
mo: 07916 74532
email: alix.smith@thcouncil.co.uk

The story:
Give me one good reason not to shut this place down right now.

Success rating:
High – but dangerous. No one wields more power or fear in the world of clubs than the council licensing officer. With one flick of your biro this place could be shut down for good in a matter of minutes. That's why the bouncers will personally take it in turns to rearrange your inner organs if they find out you're lying.

Perks:
You will be treated like the ruler of an oppressive third world regime. Anything you want – drinks, drugs, money in brown envelopes, small boys, the bloke who looked at you funny to 'disappear' – can be yours with nothing more than a raised eyebrow.

Optional props:
Clipboard, tweed suit with leather patches on elbows.

THE BUSINESS CARD BLAG

Cut out the following tried and tested designs and paste on to a good quality card or design your own. Then memorise the following stories, and you should avoid queues and charges hence forth.

No. 4 The Journalist

BEYOND NOW MAGAZINE

Alix Smith
Writer

Beyond Now
Enterprise House
259 Scruton Road
London
EC2A 4GHT

alix.s@beyondnow.co.uk
www.beyondnow.co.uk

tel:020 077 2279
mo:07916 74532

The story:
You're a writer for whatever the most fashionable magazine is this month. You have chosen to come to this night to see if it is even worth honouring in print with your hallowed words. Why are you still standing in my way?

Success rating:
Although a common manoeuvre, this can still have good results if you have the right air of disdainful authority about you. A bit of reverse psychology never goes amiss: explain that you've got to go to five other places this evening and if they really don't want you to come in then that's their loss.

Perks:
Often easy to get you and an entourage in. Once in however you are likely to be left to your own devices.

Optional props:
Clothes worn too young for your age. Clipboard with other venues listed.

DEVIL'S DANDRUFF

A reliable method of procuring free entry on the door is to pose as someone of importance. And one of the best ways to appear important is with a business card. For effective use, the cards must be accompanied by authentic patter.

No. 5   The Ambassador to Ecuador

Alix Cortez Smith
Ecuadorian Ambassador

Ecuador House
259 Scruton Road
London
EC2A 4GHT

tel: 020 077 2279
mo: 07916 74532

The story:
Prince Nahleed III is arriving next week, you are responsible for taking him to the hippest nightspots in town. Make extremely unsubtle suggestions about his wealth and generosity.

Success rating:
More successful at the higher end of the nightclubbing scale where they value your wallet more than your cool. Unlikely to cut much ice on the door at a 40 MCs / 25 DJs happy hardcore showdown. However, it is also such a far fetched and unusual request that many are likely to be so confused that they'll just let you in anyway.

Perks:
Five star treatment all the way. Any guestlist holder with an ounce of sense will realise you hold the keys to the golden goose and, depending on the stature of the venue, ply you with as much champagne/caviar/'Big D' peanuts as you can guzzle down your gob.

Optional props: Double breasted navy blue suit with gold buttons, yachting slacks, cravat.

THE BUSINESS CARD BLAG

Cut out the following tried and tested designs and paste on to a good quality card or design your own. Then memorise the following stories, and you should avoid queues and charges hence forth.

No. 6 The Pirate

Alix Smith
Pirate

Enterprise House
259 Scruton Road
London
EC2A 4GHT

*tel:*020 077 2279
*mo:*07916 74532

The story:
After travelling on stormy seas for many a month you have finally set foot on land and are looking for a knees-up full of flowing ale and lecherous wenches.

Success rating:
At certain Electro/80's revivalist nights you are likely to be whisked straight into the VIP room and showered with compliments on your daring look. Most other places though are likely to be less understanding. Sword unlikely to make it through the metal detector at Garage events.

Perks:
Saying 'arr' all night.

Optional props:
Eyepatch, big sword, bushy beard, peg leg, parrot.

DEVIL'S DANDRUFF **DOOR BLAGS**

● The Human Fly

Method: Utilising Spiderman-style suction pads climb up the wall and enter through the nearest open window.

Success rating: 9
Usefulness for getting into basement clubs: Low

Pros:
✓ Very very cool way to enter a club.

Cons:
✗ Only seems to work if you are a cartoon character robbing a bank.

● The Confident Stroll

Method: Just walk calmly in, making no eye contact with anybody, as if you obviously have every right in the world to do so. It's always worth pretending to be on a mobile phone too - you just popped out to make a call right? A slightly risky strategy but one that can often have surprising levels of success.

Success rating: 5
Potential of doing it en masse with a posse: Very small

Pros:

✓ If busted you can always claim ignorance - you didn't know where to go.
✓ A great opening blag - if it doesn't work you've always got some more moves to pull.

Cons:

✗ Harder to do than it sounds, especially if there's a big rope or bouncer between you and the entrance.

DEVIL'S DANDRUFF

The myriad species of club culture commonly congregate within five specific areas of the dancefloor. It is generally understood that the social standing and sexual magnetism of said species diminishes the further they are found from the dancefloor's core; the DJ booth.

Composite of lamb bhuna, cheap amphetamines and Red Bull.

2 for the price of 1

Likes: Watching ER re-runs Dislikes: Going to nightclubs

Trying very, very hard to remember her name

Tinnitus [Early Adopter]

Residuals:
Laggards
Drug/alchohol casualties, opportunistic thieves, 'undercover' police, bounders, cads, swells.

Outer Limit:
Latter Majoritae
Groups of unsightly females. Desperate males preying on unsightly females. Non Dancers. Snogging couples.

Secondary Ring:
Earlus Majoritae
Outer Predatory males moving in on Alpha females. Roaming drug dealer. Flamboyant dancers. Lone topless sweaty geezer.

DANCEFLOOR RINGS OF HELL

Friends of the DJ from France

Hasn't had any for the past five months, not even a suck job

**Wandering hands
Wandering body
Wandering feet**

Will attempt some very unsuccessful breakdancing moves within the next thirty minutes

Primary Ring:
Earlus Adoptae
Impossibly beautiful Alpha females and their handsome gay chaperones.

The Core:
Innovatum
Nonchalant DJ and entourage, frightening security, punters asking DJ for requests/casual sex.

DEVIL'S DANDRUFF

● Box Boy *Discus Inferius*

Having traded a university education and a safe job at Churchill Insurance for a poverty stricken disco apprenticeship, Box Boy lives a pitiful hand-to-mouth existence in the dominant shadow of his tyrannical master, the superstar DJ. Despite possessing encyclopaedic knowledge of progressive house and superior mixing skills (not to mention a substantially lower booking fee), Box Boy lacks the necessary charisma to succeed his ageing paymaster. Older examples of the species display signs of poor mental health, symptomatic of conflicting emotions of admiration and resentment towards their superstar boss. Conversation limited to (a) why the current bunch of superstar DJs are all shit ('they mix their albums on ProTools man') and (b) how great the kill switches on the new Vestax mixer are.

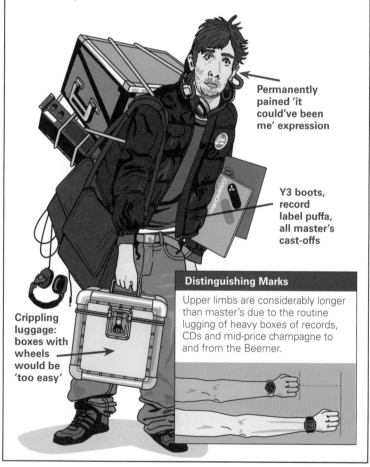

Permanently pained 'it could've been me' expression

Y3 boots, record label puffa, all master's cast-offs

Crippling luggage: boxes with wheels would be 'too easy'

Distinguishing Marks

Upper limbs are considerably longer than master's due to the routine lugging of heavy boxes of records, CDs and mid-price champagne to and from the Beemer.

● **Cloakroom Girl** *Sartorious Sultrus*

Clothed in impossibly fashionable creations of her own design, Cloakroom Girl is an emotionally fragile fashion undergraduate by day, super-spiky attendant by night. Though this species is happiest when left alone to its magical realist novel and Marlboro Reds, she will never refuse the opportunity to verbally abuse drunken customers. Having been bullied at school as the awkward goth weirdo, she now needs to 'get shit off her chest'. Occupation affords interesting opportunities to rifle customers' personal effects for useful numbers from mobile phones and the odd stick of Touche Eclat. Despite her unapproachable demeanour, Cloakroom Girl attracts myriad suitors over the course of an evening's work, but will accept advances from only the most sullen and emaciated of fashion moaners.

Designer
self-loathing

Latest necromantic
opus from Gabriel
García Márquez

Directional outfit:
Flashdance meets
Pride And Prejudice

DEVIL'S DANDRUFF

● Superstar DJ *Ego Gigas*

Despite an annual financial turnover similar to that of a small developing nation and a lifestyle similar to that of its dictator, the wildly successful Superstar DJ is beset by huge insecurity issues. Being on the top rung of an occupation that revolves entirely around playing other people's music in a more interesting order than your rivals, while lucrative, is one difficult to comprehend. With outlets for innovation at a minimum, Superstar DJ concentrates instead on expanding the financial rather than the creative side of his profession. Opportunities for artistic growth - such as learning how to actually make and produce a record - are sidelined to talented underlings due to severe attention span deficit. Soon other duties - buying records, creating mix CDs, listening to music - also become tiresome distractions from a life spent sampling the world's finest four star business hotels, and are again delegated to lower orders. Sooner or later, Superstar DJ begins to attach himself to the obvious status symbols - designer suits, flash cars, trophy girlfriends, houses with indoor snooker rooms - and his connection with the scene that made him starts to wane. Sadly for this species, the bookings eventually begin to dry up, its twilight years spent playing 'old school reunion' sets entirely off premixed CDs.

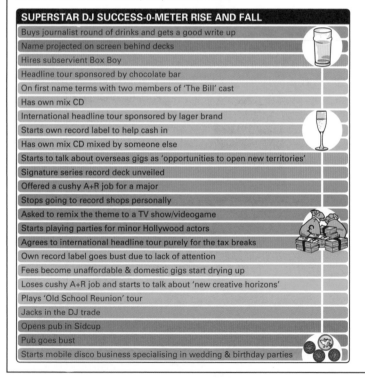

SUPERSTAR DJ SUCCESS-0-METER RISE AND FALL

Buys journalist round of drinks and gets a good write up

Name projected on screen behind decks

Hires subservient Box Boy

Headline tour sponsored by chocolate bar

On first name terms with two members of 'The Bill' cast

Has own mix CD

International headline tour sponsored by lager brand

Starts own record label to help cash in

Has own mix CD mixed by someone else

Starts to talk about overseas gigs as 'opportunities to open new territories'

Signature series record deck unveiled

Offered a cushy A+R job for a major

Stops going to record shops personally

Asked to remix the theme to a TV show/videogame

Starts playing parties for minor Hollywood actors

Agrees to international headline tour purely for the tax breaks

Own record label goes bust due to lack of attention

Fees become unaffordable & domestic gigs start drying up

Loses cushy A+R job and starts to talk about 'new creative horizons'

Plays 'Old School Reunion' tour

Jacks in the DJ trade

Opens pub in Sidcup

Pub goes bust

Starts mobile disco business specialising in wedding & birthday parties

Lucrative endorsement contract with manufacturer means headphones must be worn in public at all times

The Heathrow Airport Sunglasses Hut concession's favourite customer

Currently caning the Katie Melua album on car stereo: 'Don't want to be listening to that dance stuff when I ain't working'

Not picked up his own record box for the past two years

Mobile Phone Speed-dial
1 DJ Agent
2 Box Boy
3 Stockbroker

DEVIL'S DANDRUFF

● Promotional Cigarette Girl *Providus Venenum*

Although the appearance and manner of the *Providus Venenum* suggests a single-celled brain organism, it is often a highly complex and intelligent mammal. The primary objective of this exclusively female breed is to pass on fatal toxins and poisons to predominantly male mammals. This is most successfully achieved through utilising tools such as large breasts, tight skimpy clothing and a vocabulary in which every sentence ends with the word 'babe', 'love' or 'darling'. Commonly inhabits environments emblazoned with slogans like 'Ladies Free b4 11' and 'Vodka Jelly Shots - 2 for £2'. Research suggests these mammals show an unfathomable attraction towards relationships with unsuitable men called Tony.

Defence Mechanism

Providus Venenum stands out from other similarly marked species due to its extreme skill at seeing off predators such as the *Messius Maximus* (or 'Minesweeper') in a variety of ways.

First it will issue a playful warning sign (*Fig 1*). If this goes unheeded, she issues another, this time making the predatory party aware of her protector (*Fig 2*). If *Messius Maximus* does not pull off his attack by now, the mammal will be forced to resort to physical protection, most commonly the swift movement of walking apparatus into the predator's sexual organs (*Fig 3*).

Fig 1

Fig 2

Fig 3

DEVIL'S DANDRUFF CLUB SCUM

● Club Scum

There exists a substance found only on the dancefloors of discotheques, known commonly as 'club scum'. Jet black in colour and of a syrupy consistency, this vile substance is created from a number of by-products (see *Fig 1*) found on the dancefloor which combine over the course of an evening to become one of the toughest staining agents known to man. Its toxicity is such that delicate footwear and trouser hems are eroded on contact. The military are understood to have tested this substance for use in advanced chemical warfare.

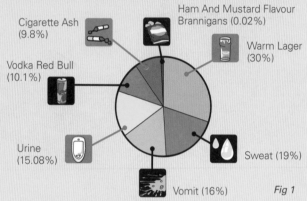

Cigarette Ash (9.8%)

Ham And Mustard Flavour Brannigans (0.02%)

Warm Lager (30%)

Vodka Red Bull (10.1%)

Urine (15.08%)

Sweat (19%)

Vomit (16%)

Fig 1

SCUM EVASION - TIPS FROM THE PROS:

★ Glue padded kitchen scourers to feet (bouncy)
★ Never leave the VIP room (poncey)
★ Wrap plastic bags around feet (thrifty) - see *Fig 2*

Placcy Bags Top Five

Fig 2

1. **Tesco Cool retro stripes**: easily available, down-at-heel chic, though liable to split.
2. **Fortnum & Mason Pea-green hue:** serves to offset this season's tweed. Thoroughbred class.
3. **Fresh & Wild Biodegradable**: so lifespan is limited, but class for pulling tofu munchers.
4. **Sainsbury's Bag For Life:** heavy duty with nice Monet painting. Bit fuddy-duddy, though, if we're honest.
5. **Iceland Clear Freezer Bags:** shows off the footwear, and brand-free. But you know yourself where they're from and it's a bit low rent, no?

BOG CONVERSATIONS

● Disco Bogs

The standard club toilet is a breeding ground not only for deadly bacteria, but for emerging relationships between fellow clubbers, united by an urgent need to evacuate bowels, consume powdered Pro Plus and steal sticks of Juicy Fruit from the professionally downtrodden attendant. Considering the random nature of liaisons with strangers in a busy toilet, conversation and behaviour stick to familiar patterns.

Common toilet queue conversation topics

● Female

1. There's never enough cubicles. Shall we go in the men's?
2. Was that bloke by the decks eyeing me up? He looks like Grant Mitchell.
3. This top isn't right, is it? Do you think I can take it back?
4. These shoes are killing me.
5. It's a fooking meat market in here.

Common toilet queue conversation topics

● Male

1. Have you seen the girl at the bar with the hooters?
2. These pills are really kicking in.
3. These pills are really weak.
4. This place is a right khazi.
5. Mate, did you just spray on my shoe?

Most common excuses for not tipping attendant

1. Fresh out of cash, mate. I'll pay you next time.
2. No CK One? Sorry, I don't wear anything else.
3. No thanks, I'll wipe my hands on my jeans.
4. (Pointing behind) Oh my god, is that Wayne Rooney? (Dashes away.)
5. I'll swap you this half pill for a Chupa Chup.

DEVIL'S DANDRUFF

● Brawler *Pikus Hardus*

Quasi-neanderthal species, seeking pleasure by extreme physical violence. City barrow boy by day, one-man maiming machine by night. Gangly, muscular physique honed on regular diet of steroid-pumped kebab meat and reassuringly expensive lager. Rarely seen dancing/smiling/having fun, preferring to intimidate weaker species, taunt security staff and tout dog-worming pills to foreign students. Capacity to consume lager and opiates matched only by complete lack of respect for any authority.

Coke bogey

Hackett polo shirt

Wife beater

Supermarket loyalty card used to rack out cheap amphetamines and disarm basic security locks

Distinguishing Marks

9ct gold-plated Argos sovereign ring/makeshift knuckle-duster, procured from recent rumble at local JD Wetherspoon.

DEVIL'S DANDRUFF

● **Undercover Policeman** *Fuzzus Covertus*

The only male in the discotheque over 50, the *Fuzzus* is immediately recognisable. Having failed in ordering 'a pint of Best please, love' he is commonly spotted propping up the bar, sheepishly sucking a bottle of Bacardi Breezer though a straw and surveying the crowd. Clothed in black nylon trousers (with crease), Bhs pullover, police-issue DMs and Smiley baseball hat, will occasionally break into a shuffle, so as not to look conspicuous. Will explain to anyone in earshot 'he's buzzing his nuts off to this tune' despite the fact he is in the chillout room while the sound tech rewires the mixer. Regularly asks punters where he can find a drug dealer to 'score some amphetamine powder or nearest equivalent'. Often befriended by said drug dealer, who will amuse himself by pointing out random innocent punters to bust while slipping narcotics into his drink. Rudimentary knowledge of club culture attained from the 'rave bust' episode of Inspector Morse. Owns every episode of Inspector Morse.

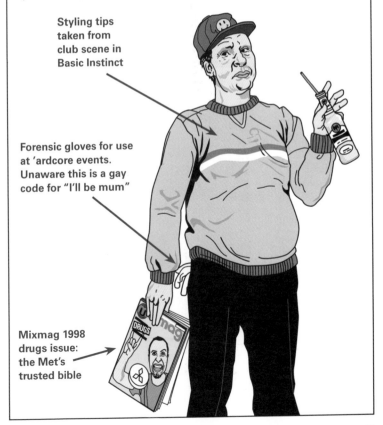

Styling tips taken from club scene in Basic Instinct

Forensic gloves for use at 'ardcore events. Unaware this is a gay code for "I'll be mum"

Mixmag 1998 drugs issue: the Met's trusted bible

DEVIL'S DANDRUFF

Vitamin D deficiency:
daylight not seen
since 1997 Brixton
Cannabis march

Style derived
from Bob Marley
football match
poster c. 1982

Digits commonly
destroyed by years
of clumsy soldering
in zero visibility

A tradesman is
only as good as
his tools, and
these are shot
to pieces

● Sound Technician *Audio Sloth*

Scrawny white rasta in super baggy T-shirt, tracky bottoms, and flip-flops (all year round). Lives off a diet of thin soggy roll-ups and lukewarm Red Stripe. Sound Technician took a BTEC in basic audio maintenance so he could live the dream of a life sat on bass bins. Originally fancied himself as a bit of a superstar DJ but 'it's just a load of posey bollocks, innit?' In reality he couldn't be arsed buying records every week and his particular brand of gabba died a decade ago. Still keeps his hand in though with a monthly set of Goa trance classics on Tuesday nights at a boozer in Brixton (bribed the landlord with cheap PA hire). Never leaves home without a mini Maglite torch, Leatherman and Cutter's Choice baccy tin. Commonly found saying, 'Nothing to do with me mate', 'Jesus! That's proper fucked' and 'I won't be able to do anything about that till Monday'. In fact, Sound Technician can normally solve any audio problem with the aid of a soldering iron, kitchen foil and a well chewed piece of Wrigley's Extra. Bit like a smelly MacGyver.

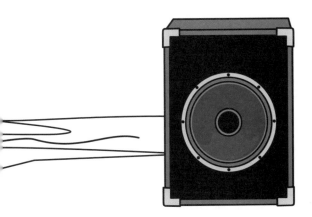

DEVIL'S DANDRUFF

All recognisable dancemoves are derived from the basic formula of connecting feet to the ground in time to the four beats of a bar of common time music (the ability to dance to non-common time music having been lost after 1958). Intricate flourishes to this formula enable the dancer to 'belong' to a Dance subculture. It is therefore inappropriate to perform 'Air Guitar' to a rolling Drum & Bass anthem.

LEGEND:

 Indicates foot on floor

 Indicates foot in air

● Trance

Jogging on the spot in time to the beat, leaning forward with a look of expectancy, arms and wrists moving backwards and forwards in unison. Curling arms, wrists and fingers in quasi-classical Indian dance style during breakdown and mouthing words with eyes closed in look of utopian ecstasy.

Optional Extra: Fish lips and trout pouts are often employed during a really 'serious' breakdown.

● Ragga/R&B

Walking in circles in time to the mid tempo beat, arms held out to the side like bird wings, with bottom stuck out and juddering fiercely in double time to the beat. Lips pursed and cheeks sucked in.

Optional Extra: The booty slap.

DANCE MOVES

● Noisy Rock

Pogoing/bounding around dance floor (see illustration) knocking into unsuspecting members of the public (at least the ones who don't look very hard), holding arms aloft towards band/DJ and making devil-horn sign with hands, occasionally breaking into air guitar moves. Basically rehashing every rock dance cliché ever made in a post-ironic bid to reconnect with youth, while trying to forget that only six months ago, rock was for acned leather-clad losers and grime was 'the thing'.

● Too packed/lazy/old to pogo

With Marlboro Red (nihilism is the key here) shoved in gob, one hand in pocket and the other holding a warm pint of Strongbow, the neck is rocked to the frenetic beat with a knowing mix of reverence and drunken abandon.

Rock style: black jeans

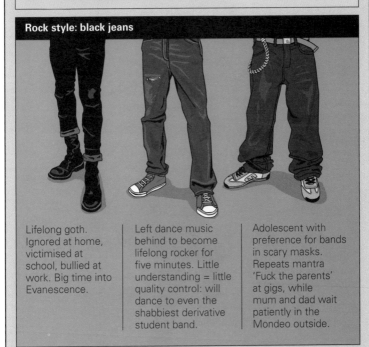

Lifelong goth. Ignored at home, victimised at school, bullied at work. Big time into Evanescence.

Left dance music behind to become lifelong rocker for five minutes. Little understanding = little quality control: will dance to even the shabbiest derivative student band.

Adolescent with preference for bands in scary masks. Repeats mantra 'Fuck the parents' at gigs, while mum and dad wait patiently in the Mondeo outside.

DEVIL'S DANDRUFF

● Whirly Git *Stinkae Windmillae*

A common sight at free festivals across the land, yet also often spotted in many urban nightspots, *Stinkae Windmillae* (known as Whirly Git) is a free spirit unencumbered by the oppressive concepts of personal space, hygiene or fashion. From the second a venue opens this creature migrates to the dancefloor, arms a-flailing and armpits a-stinking, whether the DJ is spinning the latest ATB remix or merely rewiring the stylus. Dancing to his own unique rhythms (rarely the same as those coming out of the speakers), the movements of the Whirly Git are remarkably distinctive: its arm movement akin to that of a championship bowler in slow motion, its head like that of a nodding Churchill Insurance dog, and legs like that of a 56-year-old Michael 'Riverdance' Flatley tribute act. All at the same time. Adept at spilling pints, trampling over picnics and walking straight into distressed fellow dancers. Manages to escape beatings by being commonly mistaken for the singer out of the Stereo MC's. Or someone from Stomp.

"Aromatic" homegrown skunk. Induces no high, only a headache. Still working on the formula

Burger and onion pits smell like an unwashed Starburger uniform

Beads swapped for some cheap acid at first ever Tribal Gathering

Stripey leggings not seen a washing machine since 1998

DEVIL'S DANDRUFF

● Laptop Boy *Aphex Twitus*

Ridiculously overpriced Japanese T-shirt

Used to wear a giant bright green G-Shock but wrists couldn't take the weight

Contains 37GB of tracks that all sound like badly scratched CDs of white noise

These boots were made for standing very still

Having endured uncomfortable formative years as an outsider at school, Laptop Boy continues his exclusion from mainstream adult society by refusing to attend any musical event where a four-beat kick drum is heard. Dismissing any form of music that doesn't sound like the ZX Spectrum loading tape for Manic Miner as conformist nostalgic nonsense, Laptop Boy's ears are only open to the sounds of the future. A corporate graphic designer by trade, the character dabbles in the creation of music to escape the daily drabs, though this rarely amounts to much more than putting an 808 drum loop through 20 different pirated effects programs on his PowerBook, and poring over the results for an hour. Likes going to gigs where blokes do the same sort of thing, but on stage. Last danced to a record in 1997. Majority of income spent on Japanese Planet Of The Apes toys. Currently trying to recover some credibility after his peers found, secretly hidden on his computer, ELO's Greatest Hits and a folder chock full of internet porn with Pat Butcher's face Photoshopped on.

DEVIL'S DANDRUFF

● **Stallion** *Alpha Mascula*

Though an accomplished dancer, Stallion remains relatively static at the club, observing proceedings from the peripheries of the dancefloor. This male will break into an elaborate gliding pirouette routine on sight of blonde female prey, though movement is restricted somewhat by the tightness of his Moschino trousers. Towards the final stages of an evening, the similarly tight t-shirt will be peeled off to reveal svelte musculature, to the dismay of onlooking beta males. Occasionally sipping on pricey flutes of fizz (drunken oblivion is not the objective here), promising nightcaps on sheepskin rugs, the majority of Stallion's seduction techniques are lifted from the lyrics of Omar's *There's Nothing Like This*.

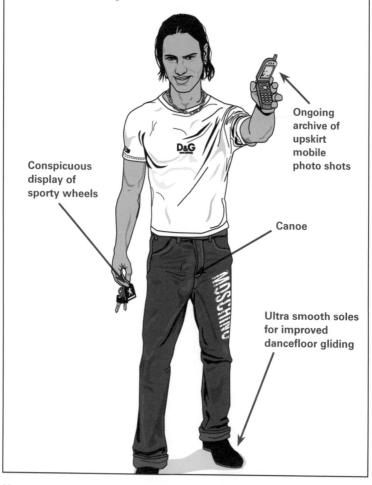

Ongoing archive of upskirt mobile photo shots

Conspicuous display of sporty wheels

Canoe

Ultra smooth soles for improved dancefloor gliding

DEVIL'S DANDRUFF

● The Straggler *Laggardum Misfortunae*

It is commonly held that, over the course of an evening, alpha males and females in the club will naturally pair early, and leave the venue to mate. It follows that the inferior species linger in the discotheque, becoming more inebriated as the search for partners becomes more desperate. Specimens found dancing to the last tune therefore tend to be physically unattractive, or simply too trashed to go home. In either case, they are incredibly frightening to early morning dog-walkers and are not to be approached under any circumstances. Feelings of rejection, status anxiety and E-induced paranoia lead this species towards morose psychobabble at the night bus-stop, turning ugly if he/she feels proper attention is not being paid.

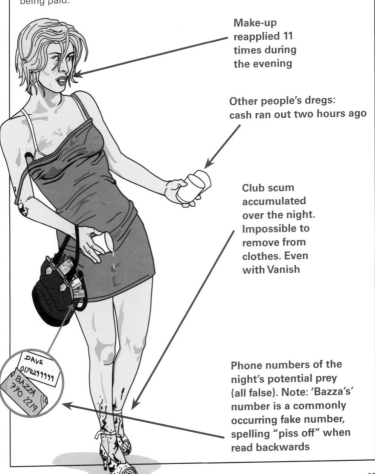

Make-up reapplied 11 times during the evening

Other people's dregs: cash ran out two hours ago

Club scum accumulated over the night. Impossible to remove from clothes. Even with Vanish

Phone numbers of the night's potential prey (all false). Note: 'Bazza's' number is a commonly occurring fake number, spelling "piss off" when read backwards

DEVIL'S DANDRUFF ANATOMY OF THE DJ BOOTH

1 Chess Timer: For the accurate timing of sets, Busy/ workshy/ pedantic DJs clock on and off on the dot, regardless of whether the next DJ has arrived to take over or not.

2 Phone Numbers: Contact numbers of people wishing to either have sex with the DJ or hire their services for a wedding reception. Usually the latter.

3 Headphones: DJs who regularly appear with brand new headphones are either (a) being paid far too much or (b) losing every other pair due to enthusiastic alcoholic consumption.

4 Dots on side of Technics: These supposedly show what speed the record is revolving at, if, for some freak reason, all the other buttons and dials that do exactly the same thing have simultaneously exploded. A bit like learning how to escape from a runaway train, it could come in handy one day, but extremely unlikely to.

5 Pitch Control: For making records go faster or slower, transforming any record from midnight stormer to erection section classic, albeit one sung by Barry White on a nasty drugs comedown.

6 EQ Knobs: For the more accomplished DJ the EQ knobs offer the opportunity to further transform the sonics of a record so that it sounds like it's coming through a 1920s gramophone, or, by continually twiddling the mid range knob, as if it was being heard through Doctor Who's

washing machine. Both these effects however are likely to clear a dancefloor quicker than a punter with an uncontrollable delhi belly so most stick to the tried and tested formula of turning the bass down and then wacking it back up again when it gets to the good bit.

PART 1

7 Crossfader: Moves the sound from record A to record B. For the novice DJ it is worth turning this off and then pretending to use it very furiously every time a record scratching solo appears in a song. At least one person in the club will be impressed.

8 Limiter: In clubs with state of the art sound systems they sometimes have a very expensive box that makes sure the music never goes above a certain decibel level. In ones without they put a bit of gaffer tape over the Master Volume control.

9 Master Volume: This makes the volume go up and down. Usually found in the 'up' position.

DEVIL'S DANDRUFF **ANATOMY OF THE DJ BOOTH**

10 **Toilet Break Record:** For those moments when the DJ really can't hold it in any longer. The 24-minute version of 'Rappers Delight' by The Sugarhill Gang is a common favourite - not only a party classic but also long enough to order a pizza, refill the parking meter, get a round in, have a quickie and still be back before the final chorus.

11 **Book (Warm Up and Chill Out DJs Only):** For when the crowd's not responding or there's no crowd at all.

12 **1p Coin on Stylus:** Often placed on stylus with bluetack/chewing gum to prevent it from jumping. Big name DJs have been known to use anything from 20p to a £1 coin. Also helps

a novice really look like they know what they're doing.

13 Fags: Well hidden from any punters on the ponce.

14 Baseball Hat/Disguise: For use when Emergency Shit Tunes CD is playing. Legend on front of hat saves DJ from responding to requests.

15 Emergency Shit Tunes CD: Many DJs spend the previous night meticulously sorting out their collection of rare techno classics into BPM order only to discover the clientele want wall to wall cheese, from Spiller though to Sister Sledge. Sensing potential violence the only way to placate the crowd is through a badly mixed set of wedding party favourites, found on this now life saving CD. If played the DJ is known to crouch beneath the console in case anyone they know pops in.

16 Selection of Booze/Drugs: For the more entrepreneurial and less professional DJ the decks also double up as a handy counter for selling home cut narcotics and booze swiped from behind the bar.

17 Mobile Phone: Usually switched off to avoid mates of mates complaining that they can't get their other ten friends in on the list and can you come and sort it out.

18 Premixed CD: Favoured by the big name DJs who, despite their exorbitant fees, really can't be arsed any more. Once playing the hour long pre-mixed CD is accompanied by an elaborate Marcel Marceau style performance over the decks and record box. Security around the DJ booth prevents any punters from getting wise and the DJ gets one step closer to the downpayment on that indoor swimming pool.

DEVIL'S DANDRUFF

● Bongo Player (Professional) *Percussiva Naseaum*

Once a colossus on the session musician scene, Bongo Player's heady days in Lisa Stansfield's backing band are now a fading memory, with only gigs playing second fiddle to overpaid young disc jockeys filling the diary. A competitive relationship exists between the pair - the Bongo Player realises that not only is he earning a quarter of the glorified jukebox behind the decks but that what he is doing is making absolutely no difference under the din of the bass bins. Despite an impressive physique, aided by a regular diet of steroids and protein powder, below-average fitness and encroaching years means that he can only perform his second-rate Latin percussion accompaniments for a total of two records at a time. The next 20 minutes between sets are spent recovering at the bar regaling female fans with anecdotes about the bassist from the Brand New Heavies and slagging off the DJ. Jealous of his success with the ladies and the godforsaken noise he is creating all over their carefully-mixed sets, purist DJs often resort to playing 'difficult' records to intimidate Bongo Player. The common result is a confused, lemming-like appreciative shuffle from the dancefloor.

Wardrobe consists entirely of cap sleeved t-shirts and aviator sunglasses

Hides declining hairline

Popular with ladies who watch WWF Smackdown

As heard on the demos for the Fine Young Cannibals' second album

Favourite joke when trying to undermine DJ's skills: One DJ says to the other 'Do you fancy going to the cinema tonight?' and the other one says 'I dunno - who's the projectionist?'

DEVIL'S DANDRUFF

● Veteran Electro DJ *Homo Technico*

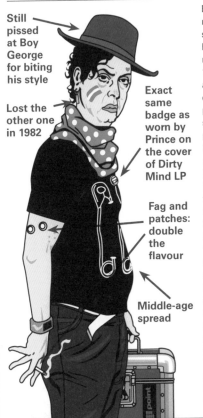

Still pissed at Boy George for biting his style

Lost the other one in 1982

Exact same badge as worn by Prince on the cover of Dirty Mind LP

Fag and patches: double the flavour

Middle-age spread

Electro DJ is among the most financially prudent of species within club culture, having not purchased a single record or item of clothing since 1987. Cleverly traversing scenes as musical trends dictate, this chameleon-like character has performed exactly the same set for two decades as a 1980s pop DJ, mid-1990s hi-NRG jock, late-1990s wedding DJ and now noughties veteran electro hero. Despite all these years of service, is still not particularly adept on the turntables, resulting in mixes often sounding like a badly wired Moog Prodigy having a bucket of cold water poured over it. 'Daring' makeup schemes and a press photo taken from the August 1992 issue of *i-D* are used to disguise the fact that his looks are no longer what they once were. Accompanied by a harem of reformed heroin addicts (all resembling Marc Almond and/or the woman from Thompson Twins), Electro DJ can recreate scenes from Desperately Seeking Susan at the most unlikely of locations.

Most Prized Possessions

● Electric blue visor with flashing pink LED effect (broken)

● Rare bootleg of music by Giorgio Moroder from The Never Ending Story II. Always a floor-filler

● Magazine signed by Wendy James of Transvision Vamp fame

DEVIL'S DANDRUFF

● The Minesweeper *Messius Maximus*

Low on funds and foresight, the *Messius Maximus* earns the nickname 'Minesweeper' from its unique habit of drinking the leftovers of any glass within sight. Having once misheard the popular saying 'wine before beer - oh dear' as 'wine before beer - no fear' the *Messius Maximus* appears to be on a one-man crusade to pour the entire product range of Threshers inside his stomach for free. Jumping from a half of lukewarm Carling (left behind speakers from previous night's club) to a discarded Lemon Barcardi Breezer (fag end swimming on top) with the grace of a 20-stone ballerina, the *Messius Maximus'* rebellion against the laws of polite society and hygiene mean that any persons he has arrived with have normally vanished within minutes. Despite crossing the not-so-fine line from being pleasantly lubricated to steamingly drunk with a great deal of success, the fatal flaw of this creature is its inability to know when to call it a night - the end of the evening is usually spent vomiting on the top deck of the night bus, blacking out and calling old girlfriends. When not drunk is most often found apologising for previous behaviour, buying Nurofen and trying to cancel lost mobile phones and credit cards.

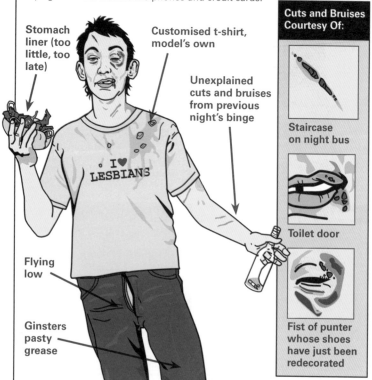

Stomach liner (too little, too late)

Customised t-shirt, model's own

Unexplained cuts and bruises from previous night's binge

I ♥ LESBIANS

Flying low

Ginsters pasty grease

Cuts and Bruises Courtesy Of:

Staircase on night bus

Toilet door

Fist of punter whose shoes have just been redecorated

DEVIL'S DANDRUFF

● Casual Carnival Queen *Liberale Opulus Patheticae*

Of all known species, Casual Carnival Queen displays the most surprising duality of character. During the majority of its annual life cycle, the breed pursues exclusively liberal bourgeois pursuits (reiki, Fresh & Wild, Zero 7) yet during the late summer, it will attempt to infiltrate the circles of society it secretly works so hard to avoid. Temporarily drawn to urban street festivals, the character will break into a poorly appropriated soca dance at the parade, occasionally shout 'Jah Rastafari' to onlooking crowds of street kids and, after sundry cans of cheap Jamaican lager, flirt with and kiss bewildered police officers. It is not unusual for Casual Carnival Queen to 'befriend' soundsystem DJs and pester them to play records by the non-threatening street pin-up Sean Paul. As night begins to fall and the customary playing of KRS One's Sound Of The Police begins, she becomes acutely aware of her vulnerability and scuttles off to the safe confines of a private members' club across town, humming refrains from Boom Bye Bye as she goes.

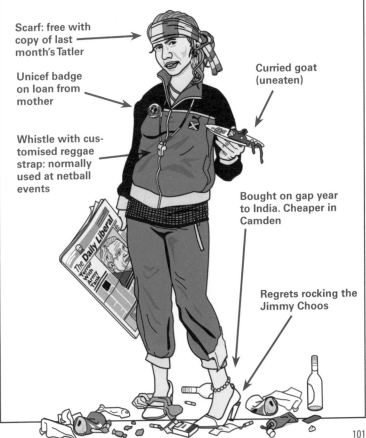

Scarf: free with copy of last month's Tatler

Unicef badge on loan from mother

Whistle with customised reggae strap: normally used at netball events

Curried goat (uneaten)

Bought on gap year to India. Cheaper in Camden

Regrets rocking the Jimmy Choos

DEVIL'S DANDRUFF

● Dad House DJ *Juvenae Deteriorum*

Commonly long of tooth, the ageing Dad House DJ has seen every type of club trend come and go (except clowncore, which was just confusing), but doggedly sticks by the hallowed purists' choice that is non-threatening, four-four soulful house. A puritanical guardian of the holy ghost of Larry Levan, he despairs of the heretic electro nonsense filling young clubbers' ears, and seeks to redress the balance by staging obscure midweek sermons on the history of disco at magnolia-coloured suburban wine bars, typically called Corks. Easily distinguished by the revived marks of 1980s casual culture (Lacoste/Tachini/Fred Perry) and the trappings of middle-age disposable income (40GB iPod with customised laser engraving/Saab estate/good quality gak chopped with Holmes Place card), Dad House DJ is spotted drinking/snorting for two on the monthly occasion he is released from babysitting duties by the despairing wife, who decided to stay at home and grow old gracefully some time ago.

Noise reduction 'phones for the hard of hearing

Entire collection begrudgingly burnt to disc - heavy records were giving his back gyp

Fair Trade Nicaraguan shot favoured over alcopops

Makeshift crèche for the thirtysomething clientele

● The Sleeper *Slumbus Unfathomabae*

The nightclub environment is composed of myriad mind-numbing stimulants for its participants to 'enjoy'. Energetic music played at deafening levels, combined with bright flashing light shows, an array of intoxicants and the possibility of casual copulation all combine to form a dynamic atmosphere. Yet one species possesses the unique capacity to kip through it all. Usually found sprawled over a bar stool, a bass bin or in a dark corner of the dancefloor, the Sleeper is inexplicably counting sheep while disco carnage continues all around. Not to be confused with the intoxicated Straggler, this character catches strategic snoozes during lulls in DJ sets, unaided by booze or downers. Eventually forming part of the evening's entertainment, Sleeper provides amusing opportunities for other bored clubbers to demonstrate their makeup skills with discarded lippy, felt tip pens and fag butts found on the floor.

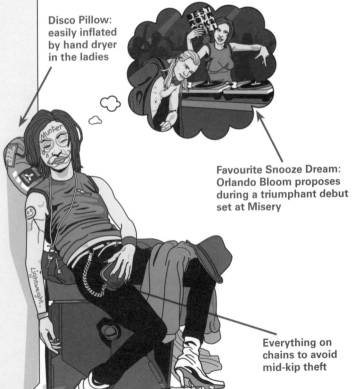

Disco Pillow: easily inflated by hand dryer in the ladies

Favourite Snooze Dream: Orlando Bloom proposes during a triumphant debut set at Misery

Everything on chains to avoid mid-kip theft

DANCE MOVES: HIP HOP

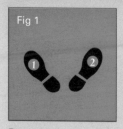

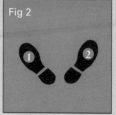

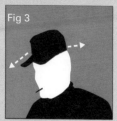

On floor   Off floor

Feet spread wide and rooted to the floor (*Figs 1 & 2*) with knees bending to the beat. Arms hanging loosely to the side, occasionally punching the air with a poorly appropriated gangland hand signal. Looking moody and sinister, mouthing key lyrics such as 'Fuck You Bitch' and 'Where's My AK-47?', taking care not to drop match stick from mouth. Violent head nodding is always appreciated (*Fig 3*).

■ Optional Extra:
Breakdancing moves are sometimes attempted with varying degrees of success. This is usually dependant upon whether dancer is (a) skilled at breakdancing or (b) drunk.

Know Your Hand Signals

Fig 1
'I feel that I am sufficiently hard to deck anybody who looks at me funnily'

Fig 2
'I'm not hard at all but I own two records by Ice T'

Fig 3
'I like getting into fights with people and losing'

Fig 4
'£20 each way on Sir Rembrandt for the 3.30 from Cheltenham'

DANCE MOVES: DRUM & BASS

Fig 1　Fig 2　Fig 3

On floor　Off floor

Bouncing uncertainly from foot to foot waving arms to stabilise. Many employ aspects of half speed Dub Reggae dancing, not to illustrate their deep understanding of the music's origin but because it's a lot less work and keeps the Air Maxs in better nick. During breakdown, shift down a gear and simply stand around nodding head. Pogo wildly when breakdown ends.

■ **Optional Extra:**
Pointing your finger in time with the music every time a big number gets played and saying 'Boo' a lot.

Tinnitus Guide

Alongside the scoring of low quality drugs, Drum and Bass nights are also an excellent place for getting hold of tinnitus. To achieve a prolonged state of hearing loss it is recommended one stands as close to the 10K speaker stack as possible during the night. Different levels of deafness can be achieved through proximity to sound source:

Not deaf at all: Kebab van outside club	Mild deafness: Ordering a drink at the bar	Might as well talk to a tree: Inside bass bin
Gene Hackman in The Conversation	Sir David Frost	Beethoven (circa 1814)

DEVIL'S DANDRUFF

Black Hole 16mm box
- swapped at a film
convention for a porno
about a German carpet
salesman

Digital is 'for
pussies'

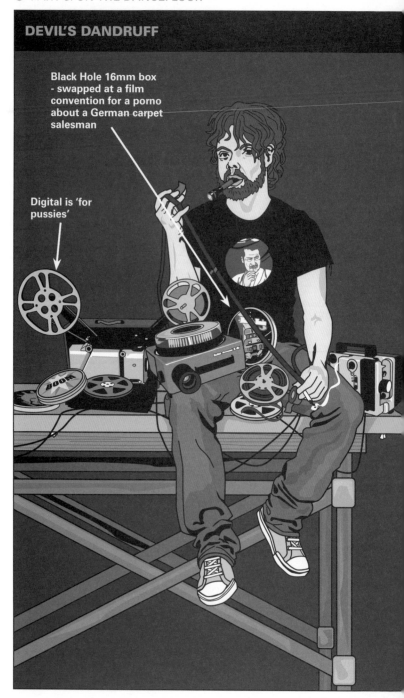

● Visuals Guy *Opticus Afflictae*

One of clubland's misunderstood geniuses, Visuals Guy creates beautiful, technically complex multimedia montages in clubs and festivals for the entire dancefloor to ignore as they drunkenly shuffle about looking at their feet. A self-proclaimed pioneer of contemporary abstract cinema, he is Hollywood's saviour in waiting. Commonly spends the majority of his waking life in the dark, smoky nether regions of the discotheque, fiddling with film/slide projectors that seem to exclusively show loops of Bruce Lee fight scenes, a nuclear bomb going off and stills from the 1986 Ferguson Videostar VHS recorder manual. From the lofty vantage point of his scaffolding, Opticus Afflictae is given to discreetly dropping greenies and fag ash on the heads of the inattentive audience. Away from the venue, he is to be found scouring film conventions and boot sales in search of the elusive 16mm print of Tron.

Favourite Trippy Visuals

2001: A Space Odyssey Astronaut Bowman journeys beyond the infinite

Vertigo The famous Saul Bass title sequence

Neighbours Jim and Doug eat magic mushrooms by mistake

DEVIL'S DANDRUFF

Over the past years a number of the great dance moves invented during the golden years of acid house and rave have slowly disappeared. Here they are again.

● The Box

One of the all time classic dance moves from the golden era of rave music, The Box is known under a myriad of names: Big Fish/Little Fish, Packing The Sandwich and Giant TV/Small Video are just a selection of names. However whilst there may be slight differences in each of these moves the basic elements remain the same, namely the use of both hands to create an imaginary box in the air. Drawing on traditions of mime the dancer will move both his hands first to the horizontal axis of the box and then to the vertical (see *Figs 1 & 2*). A more dedicated dancer will keep the palms of their hand as flat as possible in order to maximise the visual effect of the box.

Fig 1

Fig 2

Fig 3

Fig 4

● Stacking The Shelves

Another seminal dance move that is today rarely seen, Stacking The Shelves involves rapid hand movements from both the left and right arm (see *Figs 3 & 4*). With the palms held flat along the horizontal they are moved up and down with a vigourous frequency, as if the dancer was a midweek shelf stacker from Tesco who had taken too much speed. Often seen performed by a midweek shelf stacker from Tesco who had taken too much speed.

Fig 5

Fig 6

● Reach For The Sky

A not particularly exciting dance move, this usually involves the dancer slowly moving their arms up away from their body (see *Figs 5 & 6*). Certain danc- ers have been known to inject more personality into the move through also establishing a criss-cross figure of eight pattern with their arms, or simply shaking their bodies and hands as if they were a zombie off the Thriller video.

DANCE MOVES

● Hot Chips

Popular with tight repetitive tracks 'hot chips' is a move seemingly favoured only by short sweaty male dancers in beanie hats. Moving his head to the left the dancer simultaneously also raises his left hand, shaped as if it were holding a chip, and blows on it, as if to cool it down (see *Fig 7*). This move is then mirrored, the head turning the opposite way, and the right arm doing the chip-raising (see *Fig 8*). It then repeats for as long as the dancer wishes.

● Sausages

A dance move popular with anthemic, building acid house tracks. Unlike its counterparts however, this is a much more complex affair taking in a number of different moves before reaching its climactic finale.

Stage 1: Making The Sausages
The dancer moves their slightly cupped hands back and forth as if they were slowly preparing a long tube of meat (*Figs 1 & 2*). Vegetarian ravers may prefer to think of it as a giant tofu stick. This is usually found accompanying a solid four beat rhythm.

Stage 2: Cutting Up The Sausages
It is now up to the dancer to cut the long tube into a number of smaller, sausage-shaped items. The most successful way to do this is to swiftly move their hands back

and forth in a repeated up/down cutting motion (*Figs 3 & 4*). This move is usually started once a track introduces a number of stabby synthesizer or bass elements.

Stage 3: Selling The Sausages
Once the previous two stages are complete it is now necessary to 'sell the sausages' and alert potential customers. This is achieved by punching the air with a pointed finger (*Fig 5*). Some like to use both hands alternating for a greater technique (*Figs 5 & 6*). This climactic move is usually found during the chorus element of a track and is often accompanied by a slight sucking in of the cheeks or pouting of the lips.

DEVIL'S DANDRUFF

● Jimmy Choo Dealer *Beautificus Obsessionae*

The majority of species in clubland are unduly concerned with personal adornment. But for one such species, the attraction to luxury footwear and accessories is so great that she is prepared to risk life and liberty in order to possess them. Jimmy Choo Dealer is a goodtime PR girl turned small-time coke dealer, the profits of which are spent solely on extravagant, high-heeled, fuck-me shoes. The value placed on footwear is such that *Beautificus Obsessionae* is rarely sighted close to the dancefloor, or the bar for that matter, opting for VIP areas where potential customers are more wealthy and there is less danger of scuffage to the kitten heels. As the night's gack consumption wears on (the old Scarface adage 'Never get high on your own supply' long forgotten), friends and acquaintances begin to resemble walking LV bagettes, talking Dior belts; every customer taking her £50 closer to a Chloe clutchbag. Working the room, she is every girl's bessie mate, every male's fantasy shag, yet she returns home alone, to rearrange the extensive collection of Westwood costume jewellery, plus the half-hourly rail of horse tranquilliser.

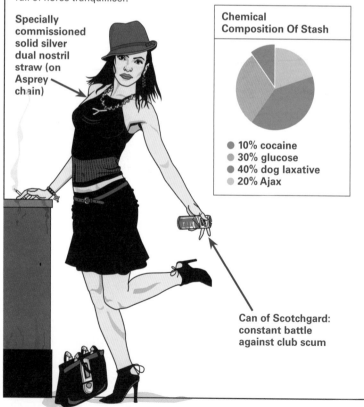

Specially commissioned solid silver dual nostril straw (on Asprey chain)

Chemical Composition Of Stash

● 10% cocaine
● 30% glucose
● 40% dog laxative
● 20% Ajax

Can of Scotchgard: constant battle against club scum

● Fancy Dress Fanatic *Seekus Attentionae*

New Year's Eve, Halloween, the passing of exams, the finding of a 10p piece down the sofa. For one species, any minor event in life is an excuse to celebrate. And a key celebratory technique for *Seekus Attentionae* is the donning of ostentatious, humiliating costumes. Rabbit ears and freckles at Easter, French maid gear at hen nights, tiaras and fairy wings at new year; any notions of self respect are out the window, every dress code in the bouncer's book is broken, as the gaggle of good-time party people push their way past the door (having block-booked previously so they can't be turned away) and singlehandedly shatter any notions of sophistication on the dancefloor. Less euphoric punters become confused (it's too miserable to sneer but too embarrassing to join in) and instantly disperse to safer enclaves of the club. Fancy Dress Fanatic is a direct descendent of Office Comedian with the 'I'm mad, me' novelty tie and socks. Both related species, though refreshingly free from pretension, possess the power to shatter cool at 30 paces.

Fixed grin: 'You will appreciate my outfit and comedy dancing'

Bare flesh: sub zero temperatures not an issue

Angel dust: toxic glitter thrown in the face of uncharitable strangers

DEVIL'S DANDRUFF

● Toilet Attendant *Guiltus Instillae*

There are few species that instil trepidation as much as the *Guiltus Instillae*. On his appearance the primary objective of many a mammal will instantly alter. No longer will they be concerned purely with relieving themselves; now they must engage in a stealthy game of eye contact avoidance, timing and furtive hand cleaning. While many in the species play the role of mute manservant in the vague hope of a guilt-ridden financial reward, the more canny occupy themselves in light-hearted banter with their prey. By quickly establishing a bond, however meaningless, the prey is temporarily blinded to their situation and in a flash is squirted with soap and handed a paper towel. Although these are all acts easily performed by even the most

Target demographic: idiots or person with stolen phone

WIN BIG WIN NOW
BAR BAR BAR
WIN BIG @
www.numbnutcasino.com

Text me

Stopped pissing a minute ago - now just waiting for other bloke to finish and divert attention of attendant

incapable of mammals the rattling of a plate of pound coins signifies that *Guiltus Instillae* expects reward for this ludicrously mundane task. At this point the prey has two options - (a) make a run for it or (b) grudgingly dig deep into their pockets, asking for a squirt of deodorant to help justify the financial outlay. Neither party is rarely able to leave the situation with their dignity intact. The more experienced toilet user however often waits for a 'patsy' to take up the time of *Guiltus Instillae* before pissing at breakneck speed and nipping out without washing their hands.

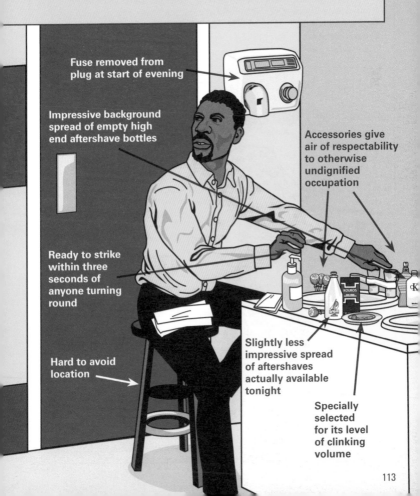

Fuse removed from plug at start of evening

Impressive background spread of empty high end aftershave bottles

Accessories give air of respectability to otherwise undignified occupation

Ready to strike within three seconds of anyone turning round

Hard to avoid location

Slightly less impressive spread of aftershaves actually available tonight

Specially selected for its level of clinking volume

DEVIL'S DANDRUFF

● Disco Mum *Hotticus Flushae*

Recently divorced and newly liberated, Disco Mum can be spotted out on the town 'chaperoning' her younger (often underage) daughter in a bid to recapture lost youth. While a symbiotic relationship exists between the pair (she bribes the bouncers and buys the Frexienet, the daughter provides social interaction with anyone under the age of 35), it is an uneasy one; the lecherous men she is so keen to meet are only interested in mauling her offspring. Hailing from the Donatella Versace school of make-up ('More is more') and sporting an outfit that is one part Tina Turner (c. 1989) to three parts Cosmo Girl, personal style is perhaps not her strong point. Despite the obvious attractions of her daughter, Disco Mum finds herself a big hit with certain men, and once a suitor who lives up to the suitable requirements is met (any male under 45 with a full set of teeth and a car that's C-reg or above), the rest of the evening is spent tongue-wrestling him in a darkened corner of the dancefloor.

Silvikrin hair spray: avoid contact with naked flames and airborne insects

Only UK resident still wearing leather strides. Except Nicky Clarke. And Jeremy Clarkson

Accessories: daughter's hand-me-ups

Key Brands

● **New Look:** young affordable fashion with an adult twist for mums on the go.

● **Louis Vuitton:** via the local market.

● **Ernest & Julio Gallo:** lower mid range vino more sophis than Smirnoff Ice.

● **Menopace:** keeps the hot flushes at bay.

● The Breakdancer *Atmospherus Massacarae*

Aside from the DJ spinning Barcelona by Freddie Mercury during a pumping breakbeat set, there are few things that will kill the mood on the dancefloor with greater speed than the arrival of *Atmospherus Massacarae*. After he's marked his territory with five minutes of "toprocking" (a move that looks like a very confused man running on the spot), the crowd will eventually stop dancing and form an uninterested circle around him. After continuing this motion for a couple more minutes (a consummate showman, breakdancer knows the key to entertainment is building suspense), he will eventually fall to the floor, spin around a bit, wobble his body, stick his arms underneath his legs and waddle about. Arising to a muted round of applause, *Atmospherus Massacarae* will then quickly nip off to the toilets to neck half a pack of Nurofen before returning, Aertex top removed, to mingle with the now much more subdued party people. Supplements income with weekend robotics show outside the local greengrocers.

Related Species

Jazz dancer   Ex-ballet dancer   Rubbish salsa couple

Still gets mum to press his tracksuits

As worn by Hightower in the breaking scene of Police Academy 4: Citizens On Patrol

Local chiropractor number on speed dial

DEVIL'S DANDRUFF

● DJ Bird *Trophus Devotae*

The role of DJ Bird is one of complicated contradictions. Inside the DJ booth, she must play the trophy wife, while avoiding bimbo status. She must refresh the booze rider and carry equipment (no more than the headphones), but she is no doormat. She must appear nonchalant at all times, but feverishly ward off rival females from the decks. All the while battling with the realisation that DJs are glorified trainspotters who are good at playing other people's records (a job she could easily do better herself). After years of playing second fiddle, more mature examples of this species have been known to muscle in on their man's performance, Linda McCartney style, playing tambourine or even scatting along to the repetitive beats. The craving of limelight aside, DJ Bird adheres to the Tammy Wynette school of coupledom, standing by her man at the decks, even when he's cleared the floor with an electro remix of Ghostbusters.

'Special Agent' stare - continually scanning the room for potential female predatory attacks on partner

Can keep same slow, slightly unenthusiastic body-bobbing going for an entire eight-hour set

● **Club Journalist** *Scribblus Parasitus*

Alongside Venue Owner and Licensing Officer, the rarely sighted Club Journalist sits high atop the nightclub food chain, and exerts very little energy to maintain such exalted status. Making or breaking the careers of Promoters and DJs with the click of a mouse, *Scribblus Parasitus* bases his valued opinions less on the tireless attendance of discos the world over and more on a combination of boozy lunches (courtesy of Promoter), 'reinterpreting' press releases and Mystic Meg-style predictions based on the way the wind blows that day. Such are his visionary powers that Club Journalist can dictate the pace of club culture from the luxury of the VIP room, without setting foot on a dancefloor for long periods of time. With the need to attend smelly nightclubs all but eradicated, this cunning breed prefers to spend evenings buzzing around the nesting grounds of Superstar DJs or enjoying the launch hospitality of the latest alcopop.

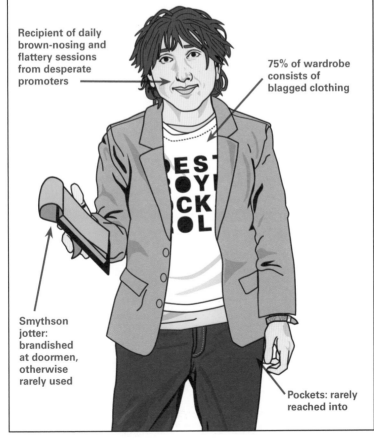

Recipient of daily brown-nosing and flattery sessions from desperate promoters

75% of wardrobe consists of blagged clothing

Smythson jotter: brandished at doormen, otherwise rarely used

Pockets: rarely reached into

DEVIL'S DANDRUFF

● Sweaty Top Off Dancer *Perspiritus Irritus*

Nightclubs are commonly hot, dank, sweaty environments, where, thanks to the stinginess of Venue Owner, the only concession to any sort of air conditoning is keeping the bog windows ajar. The majority of species attending the disco will thus spend an extraordinary amount of time and money safeguarding against sweaty pits, face and back with sprays, lotions and breathable outer gear. All except for *Perspiritus Irritus*, who positively revels in it. Although an enthusiastic consumer of unmarked 'mystery' pills he refuses to wear any deodorant on the dubious grounds that its man-made chemicals would pollute his body. Which is unfortunate as this breed seeps fluid like a blocked up urinal; indeed if he were to attend a mid morning open-air nudist disco in Iceland, he would still perspire. In the more familiar surroundings of the suburban nightclub, he becomes drenched on immediate contact with the dancefloor, compelled to strip to the waist, revealing a wiry sweat-soaked torso. As the dancefloor fills to capacity and the beats become more hypnotic, *Perspiritus'* movements become more elaborate and so begins another night of brushing uncontrollably against appalled punters who fear for their own odour/hygiene/dry cleaning bill. This appalling social faux pas is amplified by the steadfastly positive, gregarious nature of the species; offering drinks, cigs and the occasional hug to all that surround him, it is impossible for the average breed to pluck up courage and ask him to piss off. A distant cousin to Straggler, Sweaty Dancer is oblivious to concepts of time and space, and will be found dancing in a pool of salty water, right up to the last triumphant tune. Note: for reasons as yet unknown, the female variant of this species is far less repellent to the opposite sex, particularly when found dancing in fluffy bra or halter neck top (see Professional Clubber).

No man's land: safe distance for dancers wishing to remain dry

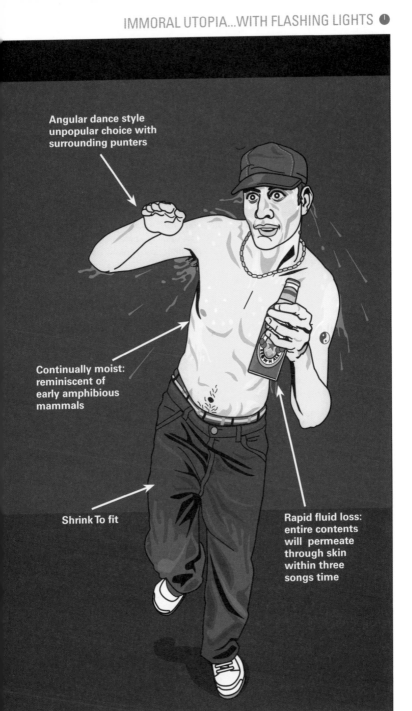

Angular dance style unpopular choice with surrounding punters

Continually moist: reminiscent of early amphibious mammals

Shrink To fit

Rapid fluid loss: entire contents will permeate through skin within three songs time

DEVIL'S DANDRUFF

● **Promoter** *Prospero Disingenuae*

Despite occupying a position that many regard as glamorous, the daily routine of Promoter is fairly mundane; lugging heavy boxes of flyers across town, brown-nosing journalists, booking DJs, getting stupid haircuts and finding new floorboards in the office to hide cash under are all standard weekday activities. Come the 'big night' however, and the promoter must have the characteristics of a chameleon. While sporting a set of symbols that, to many, display success (flashy wheels, overpriced trainers and copious nosebag) to their closest confidantes (who strangely are always the same people owed money by said promoter), the species rarely sings anything other than the sorriest of hard luck tales. An accounting virtuoso, well versed at playing Rachmaninov on the club cash register, Promoter is able to turn any successful evening into an apparent financial disaster. DJs get fobbed off with loose change, bouncers are handed rubber cheques and staff are given the saddest of sob stories. To be found escaping out of the toilet window halfway through the night, with pockets stuffed full of used notes.

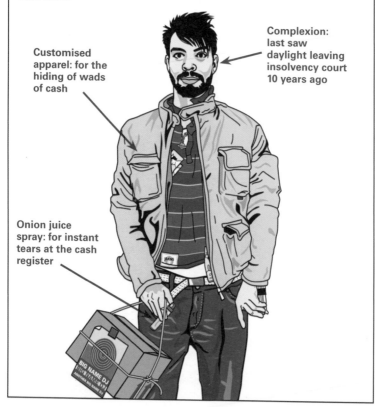

Complexion:
last saw
daylight leaving
insolvency court
10 years ago

**Customised
apparel:** for the
hiding of wads
of cash

**Onion juice
spray:** for instant
tears at the cash
register

● Fat White Hip Hop DJ *Glutinous Beatus*

Wide in girth but thin on conversation *Glutinous Beatus* prefers to let his selection of music define his personality. Playing a tightly mixed set of exclusively American Gangsta hip-hop tracks *Glutinous Beatus* is often under the illusion that he himself is a gun-totin', bitch pimpin', drug dealin' OG rather than simply an overweight 28-year-old who still lives with his mum in Surbiton. An obsessively anal dedication to mastering obscure scratching techniques, frequently demonstrated to frustrated clubbers, and a ridiculously dismissive attitude to any other form of music not reviewed in *The Source* are cornerstones, in his eyes, to proving his realness to fellow hip-hoppers. Has been to New York once on a rap sightseeing tour. Still dreams of the day he can feel confident enough to call his fellow colleagues 'niggas'.

Gripmaster: heard that DJ Q-Bert used one to develop his hand muscles

Bought with Argos gift vouchers from Gran

3 Most Embarassing Moments:

1. Forgetting swimming trunks at primary school

2. Caught wanking by his mum

WILL SMITH
WILD WILD WEST

3. MC mate discovering his hidden stash of Will Smith 12"s

Get ready for 5 minutes of tedious scratching noises

One size fits two

Needles: always brings his own

DEVIL'S DANDRUFF

● DJ Stalker *Trainspottus*

Worshipping at the altar of Superstar DJ, *Trainspottus* appears at every date in his idol's diary; a motionless figure timidly hovering around the DJ booth from start to finish of every event. DJ Stalker's sole obsessive objective in life is to record the title of every record spun by his chosen God. A lonely species with stunted inter-personal skills, *Trainspottus* never summons the courage to communicate with Superstar DJ, preferring instead the occasional nod of recognition. This complete devotion leads to the acquiring of an identical record collection to his peer, an occupation which leaves few funds available for non-essential items such as clothing. As a result this species is often shabbily dressed. DJ Stalker's continual presence at the booth is an increasing irritation to Superstar, who prefers the half naked female variety of fan to this shabby nuisance. A devotional website built by Stalker, exhaustively listing every set his hero has ever played causes further frustration, as it unintentionally exposes the remarkable simularity of Superstar's extortionately expensive sets. As a result, the deity takes to sticking blank white labels over the names off all tracks played.

Never more than 5 feet away from the DJ booth

Phone bill costs increased exponentially since discovering 2580 Shazam

Entire outfit, including shoes, actually cheaper than a recently purchased rare bootleg 12"

Great Leaders

Throughout history the charisma and conviction of certain leaders has inspired their followers to equally great works of art:

Jesus Christ
Da Vinci's painting of The Last Supper

Mahatma Gandhi
'Gandhi - The Film'

Superstar DJ
Darren's Banging House Mix Vol 2

● Wall Hugger *Columno Stickus*

Years of contact with cold concrete has resulted in severe rectal complaints

Multiple finger props

No matter how rocking a party the *Columno Stickus* will rarely stray from its favoured position, that of leaning against a wall on the edge of the dancefloor. The species is also found to heavily populate bar areas and posts. Once its territory is marked it is seldom left, save for the occasional trip to the toilet or fag machine. Believing that dancing would somehow undermine his fashionable air of nonchalance *Columno Stickus'* physical exertions are seldom greater than the occasional head nod and beer chug. This cool demeanour however is merely a front for a personality that has yet to progress beyond the social dynamics of the school disco: 'tis better to do nothing than make a fool of oneself by having a good time'. As he coolly scans the dancefloor the mammal is under the misguided impression that, once the other males have disgraced themselves through their ludicrous styles of dancing, his sheer presence in the room will emit enough charisma to ensure he will be beating women off with a stick. Despite this the species rarely registers on the female radar and by the end of the night the only person doing the beating off is usually himself.

Perfected a style of one foot dancing (even to Drum & Bass) while the rest of the body remains inanimate

DEVIL'S DANDRUFF

● Professional Clubber *Fluffus Brassierus*

If ever there was a species closest to the impossibly utopian imagery
found on club flyers (see Club Flyers Explained, page 27), it is
the Professional Clubber. Humdrum secretarial PA by day, sparkly
dancefloor diva by night, she is the eternally bubbly good time party girl;
immaculately attired in this week's high street trends with twenty Silk Cut
in one hand, designer tipple in the other. An attractive species with home
counties good looks and a limitless supply of positive energy, *Fluffus
Brassierus*'s years of disco experience enables her to avoid the unsightly
pitfalls of debauchery with incredible skill. Lesser mortals will be leading
gurning competitions, showering the floor with sweat or inspecting the
dancefloor close up, face down, while Pro-Clubber is shimmying on the
podium fresh as a daisy, well aware of her power as the object of every
E'd-up male's fantasy. Such is her value on the dancefloor that *Fluffus
Brassierus*'s standing often rises beyond that of mere punter. Blowing
kisses for club photographers at every opportunity, she regularly
appears in the back pages of Mixmag, and as an extra in generic
clubbyTV adverts for brands that wish to be 'down with the kids'. Such
antics are quickly seized upon by Promoter (adept at exploiting free
promotional opportunities) who upgrades her status to resident dolly
bird complete with free entry for her sexy mates, one shot of house
vodka and an extremely tight t-shirt emblazoned with the event's logo
over the tits. Before long, Pro-Clubber becomes the unofficial host of the
venue, befriending the staff, Venue Owner and half of the clientele, until
Promoter's status anxiety kicks in and she is banned from the club.

Pro-clubbing Outfits Through The Ages

1980s: fluffy bra/ bikini top

1990s: novelty micro t-shirt with flashing LEDs

2000s: barely there scarf top

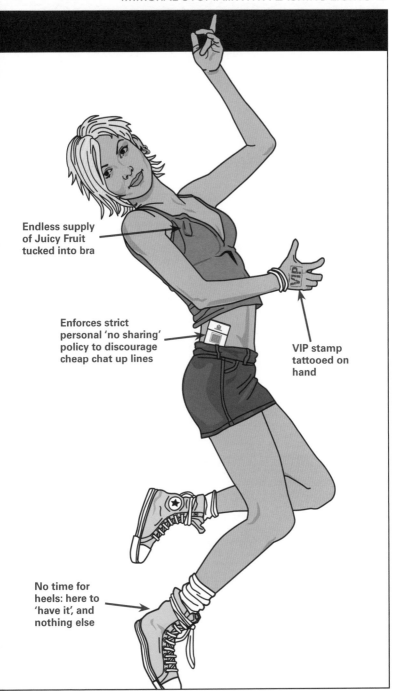

Endless supply of Juicy Fruit tucked into bra

Enforces strict personal 'no sharing' policy to discourage cheap chat up lines

VIP stamp tattooed on hand

No time for heels: here to 'have it', and nothing else

PART 4: POST DISCO

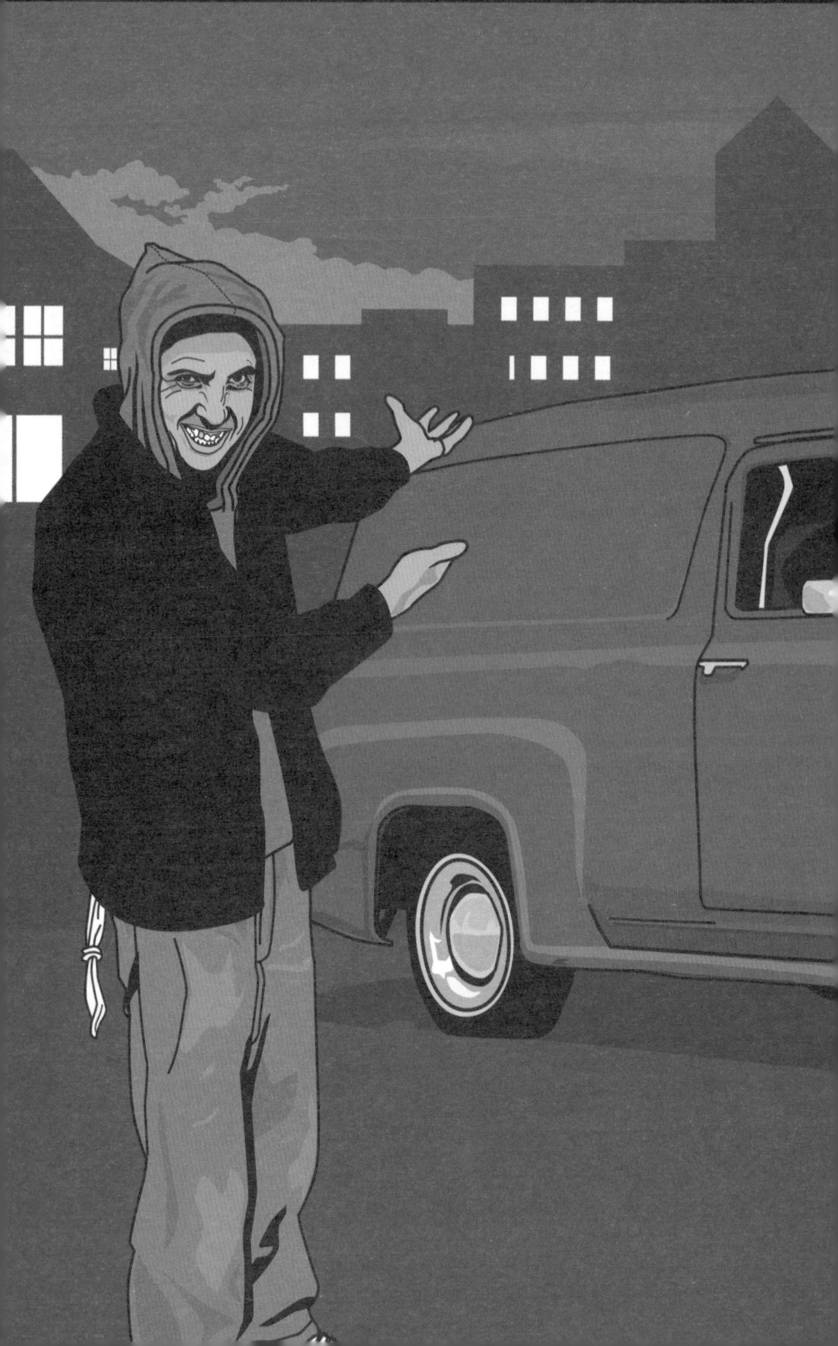

DEVIL'S DANDRUFF

Ways of Getting Thrown Out

While certain establishments may pride themselves on the difficulty it takes to gain admittance into their hallowed quarters they are rarely so choosy or slow to act when it comes to ejecting individuals.

Contrary to the 'anything goes' attitude perpetuated on flyers, most nightclubs are home to unwritten draconian laws that, on a whim, allow staff to eject anyone with scant regard for recourse or appeal.

IMPROMPTU MC PERFORMANCE

Benefits: 9
You get to give your mates shout outs and demonstrate to the entire club your microphone mastery. Or lack of. Your brazen lack of respect for both performers and nightclub etiquette will even warm the heart of even the most jaded punter.

Damage: 3
Nothing too serious, unless of course you incited a call to arms with your requests for everyone to 'bum rush the barman'. A clip round the ear from the bouncer. DJ unlikely to be receptive to future record requests.

Ease: 3
Watchful security, large stages and a confusing mixing desk set-up make this a tricky one to predict. Your chances of success are in the hands of the gods.

DRIVING A MOTORCYCLE INTO THE MIDDLE OF THE DANCEFLOOR

Benefits: 10
You get to recreate one of your favourite childhood celluloid moments – that bit in Weird Science where the motorcycle gang drive around the house party - that will be talked about in awed tones by your contemporaries for decades to come.

Damage: 10
An appearance in court, a large fine, and quite possibly, if the judge is in a bad mood that day, a bit of time doing porridge. The latter alone could subsequently lead to a number of unprovoked beatings & a funny John Wayne-style walk courtesy of your new 'daddy'.

Ease: 1
Not only will you have to procure a large motorcycle that you are willing to have confiscated but you will also have to do research into the architectural layout of a venue and have a number of associates on the inside to assist your entry with the opening of emergency exit doors & so on. For the hardcore only.

DEVIL'S TRUMPS

STARTING A FIGHT

DEVIL'S TRUMPS

Benefits: 4
You get to prove your physical superiority and/or settle an argument 'the old fashioned way' (i.e. like a neanderthal caveman with shit for brains). Possibly will impress certain bystanders by demonstrating your distaste for long winded verbal negotiation.

Damage: 7
Common sense dictates trying it on only with those convinced you could 'have'. If however you are squaring up to someone quite hard, doing it in full view of security will ensure only limited damage as any fights will hopefully be swiftly broken up. You may be escorted from the premises but you will do so with your dignity, & most of your bones, intact.

Ease: 10
As easy as pouring a pint of beer over someone's head then spitting in their face.

SELLING COUNTERFEIT DRUGS

Benefits: 8
Who would have thought a £1.49 pack of peppermint flavoured Rennies could make you over £60 in under an hour? Added bonus over selling real drugs is not only are they cheaper and easier to procure but the Police can't pin as much on you if rumbled.

Damage: 9
If caught by venue – ejected and possibly turned over to the rozzers. If caught by previous customers unlikely to be thanked for their now settled stomachs. A high risk strategy with poor odds on you not leaving the evening without some kind of low level violence inflicted.

Ease: 7
There are few jobs that have lower barriers to entry than this. All you need is to wander around the club whispering 'pills pills' to anyone who looks like they're on freshers' week at the local uni. Your success rate is dependant on your appearance – the shiftier the better.

UNWANTED SEXUAL MOLESTATION

Benefits: 5
A crowded dancefloor provides the ideal camouflage for cheap feel-ups for the sexually starved male.

Damage: 5
Depends on how careful you've been. Anything from a slap round the face to a full scale beating if you've been mistakenly pinching the bouncer's arse throughout the duration of the latest bootleg cut up of 'That's The Way I Like It'.

Ease: 7
The jostling, chaotic nature of the dancefloor provides the perfect smokescreen. Incidents can be easily blamed on other individuals, getting pushed about by the crowd, or, if you are feeling particularly adventurous, role researching for your local amateur dramatic society's staging of 'Dirty Dancing'.

DEVIL'S TRUMPS

DEVIL'S DANDRUFF

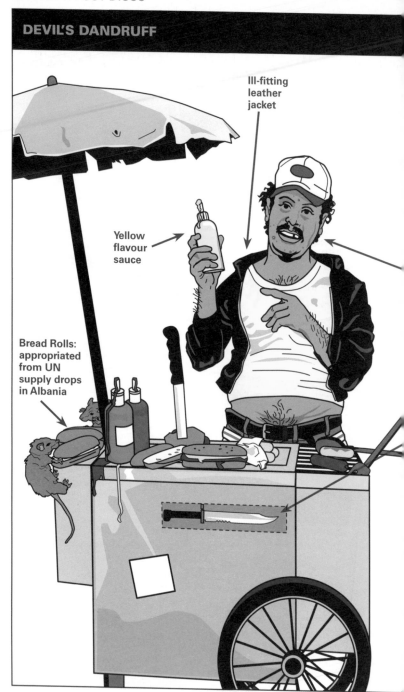

Ill-fitting leather jacket

Yellow flavour sauce

Bread Rolls: appropriated from UN supply drops in Albania

● Hot Dog Merchant *Cheapus Meatus*

Most commonly found inhabiting areas heavily populated by minicab touts (*Drivus Badlyae*) and inebriated youngsters. Often drawn towards vomit-covered pavements, a good indication of opportunities for the mammal's primary objective: the selling of undercooked meat-like sausages and burnt onions to intoxicated men (*Lecherous Maximus*) who have failed to find a mate for the evening. Although slow (the symbiotic relationship with the *Trolley Rusticus* hampers any fast travelling speeds) the *Cheapus Meatus* is highly mobile and able to turn up at a gathering of drunken people within minutes. Years of exposure to stale meat has enabled the mammal to build up a unique genetic structure, one fully resistant to any form of food poisoning. As a result it shows a flagrant disregard for sell-by dates and hygiene laws.

Special onion grease acne

Stabbing knife (hidden in trolley)

Other Late Night Snack Options

● **Pasties and rolls:**
Friendly, healthy looking packaging disguises the fact that most of these products contain exactly the same ratio of minced rats' noses, cow hoofs and horse lips as a street hotdog.

● **Crisps:**
After hours any outlets left open only seem to stock special 'Grab Bag' size - same amount of crisps but bigger packet and twice the price.

● **Cheese Strings:**
For the more gourmand late night snacker these chewy plastic dairy by-products are frequently a popular choice.

COMMUNICATION

Unlike most mammalia, the *Cheapus Meatus* enjoys a limited vocabulary, usually restricted to the following phrases:

★ *'Hot dog, hot dog'*
★ *'Two pounds, chief'*
★ *'You need minicab?'*
★ *'I can get you other stuff'*
★ *'Go see my man over there'*

● Flyer Distributor *Insomnius Beleaguerus*

The phrase 'long suffering' was surely invented for Flyer Distributor, the promotional foot soldier that stands in the howling wind and rain night after night, watching everyone except himself have a good time. Enduring sleep depravation, progressive pneumonia and tedium beyond compare, *Insomnius Beleaguerus* sticks doggedly at his post (the arse end of a nightclub) in order to hand out flyers to disinterested and drugged up clubbers. With the handouts promising hours upon hours of nocturnal utopia most promoters would rather hire a stylishly-attired sexy model to supervise distribution. Unfortunately the acute awfulness of the work means that *Beleaguerus*, a pale grizzly wreck of a man in thirty odd layers of second-hand goretex and fleece, is the only one desperate enough for the job. Considering Flyer Distributor has witnessed so many two-bit chancers transform themselves into successful club impresarios it is a wonder that he never crossed the career line into promotion himself. This mystery is perhaps best explained by the demoralising contents of his car's back seat (a distributor's home from home), a veritable smorgasbord of Pro Plus Extra tablets, Pot Noodles, prescription steroids and 3 for 2 value packs of well-thumbed jazz mags. There is a method to this species' kamikaze madness though. Unbeknownst to his employers, he will soon begin a new, opulent life in Rio De Janeiro; the result of a long-standing deal with a major paper recycling plant and the drip feeding of 10,000,000 undelivered bits of promotional paper.

Rigor mortis smile modelled on that of Tony Blair's

Capable of withstanding stress positions that would make the SAS cry for mummy

Bought off a shifty bloke in the pub

Jobsworth security ensure threshold is never, ever crossed

DEVIL'S DANDRUFF

Very few
promotional
Chupa Chups
are ever actually
distributed

DEVIL'S DANDRUFF

Promoter

Stung by ever increasing DJ bills, Promoter has to come up with a sure-fire way of enticing more punters through the door. Despite considering a number of novel and daring schemes to increase awareness amongst the target demographic all are rejected for potentially taking up more than an hour of Promoter's time. He thus instead decides to print 20,000 flyers for the 500 capacity venue in the vague hope that someone who sees one might want to come.

Printer

In the depths of a windswept, out of town industrial estate Promoter is offered a backhanded deal from Printer to produce an additional 80,000 flyers for a minimal extra charge. Cash is exchanged and the Promoter congratulates himself for yet another inspired business decision. On delivery however, Promoter realises he has nowhere to store such a ludicrously large number of flyers. The rest of the evening is spent driving round in a van with its number plates removed looking for a secluded spot to dump two thirds of said stock.

Flyer Distributor

One of the keys to successful advertising is capturing an audience at their most receptive. The majority of people leaving a nightclub however seem rarely concerned about the planning of next week's social engagements. It is thus the job of the flyer distributor to thrust as many pieces of unwanted paper at them as possible in the vague hope that they stick some of them in their pockets, to be rediscovered at a later date. The majority of these communiqués however are casually glanced at and then swiftly discarded in the street.

THE CLUB FLYER INDUSTRY: HOW IT WORKS

Paper Supplier

On learning of Promoter's decision, a large, leathery-skinned man on the other side of the world cuts down half an acre of prime Amazonian rainforest with a chainsaw. This area is then cleared to make way for cattle destined to sizzle on a kebab spit somewhere in Manchester. After receiving a financial settlement for his land (roughly equivalent to the price of a multipack of McCoys crisps) the man forlornly fondles his oversized moustache and cries inside for the future of his children.

Flyer Designer

Briefed to create an eye-catching visual identity for the upcoming event, Flyer Designer works through the night to create a stunning Photoshop montage of 18th century Impressionist landscapes juxtaposed with urban imagery of 1960s tower blocks. The artwork's subtle references to Le Corbusier, Erno Goldfinger and Sartre though cut little ice with the Promoter and it is swiftly rejected. The next draft however, featuring the name of the headline DJ in giant 50 point bold type above a picture of a bird with big tits licking her finger, is accepted.

Street Cleaner

In order to maintain the Music & Dance license, Venue Owner pays an extortionate monthly fee to the local council to clear the streets of the weekly flyer mountain. Possibly one of the hardest working members of their workforce, Street Cleaner receives only a miniscule percentage of this charge. The rest is spent on extravagant spreads of Danish pastries for councillor's morning meetings and countless bottles of Mr Sheen for the daily polishing of the Mayor's gold chains.

DEVIL'S DANDRUFF

It is understood that the only reason clubbers stay out past midnight is the possibility of sex or drugs or both. Thus the dying embers of a disco are rarely a glamorous affair. The lights go up, the final record runs out (typically *As* by Stevie Wonder), and the bouncers encircle the floor, ready to herd any

● The Optimist

Parting gesture:
'All back to mine.'

Intention:
An evening of unbridled passion with two sexually charged glamorous females.

Actual result:
Some unknown geezer falling asleep on the sofa having worked his way through the Twiglets.

● The Pessimist

Parting gesture:
Threatening the bouncers.

Intention:
Crumbling in under such a worthy physical and mental opponent, said bouncers agree to ignore all licensing laws and keep venue open for another five hours.

Actual result:
Physical ejection towards the vicinity of the bins.

last hopefuls towards the exit. Expectations not met, the sting of rejection, the dawning of the truth that less exciting times are round the corner, all call for one final parting gesture.

● The Realist

Parting gesture:
The dejected stroll off.

Intention:
Casually bumping into another exciting soirée on the way home.

Actual result:
On the nightbus, alone, trying to avoid eye contact with the unhinged, pissed-up tramp cruising the aisle.

● The Pissed

Parting gesture:
Telling everyone how beautiful they all are and how much you love them.

Intention:
That the evening will never end and you will all be friends forever.

Actual result:
Crying all the way home in an extortionately overpriced minicab.

DEVIL'S DANDRUFF

● Fast-Food Loser *McTragic III-Fatus*

The success of an evening's clubbing is dependent on a number of variables; meeting companions at the right time and place, gaining entry at the door, and not being thrown out early. Failure of the above leads to an early train home, and during the wait for said train, a visit to the nearby fast-food emporium. This is where we find the Fast-Food Loser, an unlucky breed of clubber that spends more time chewing on the Colonel's Crispy Chicken Strips than dancing to repetitive beats. Lost, stood-up, denied entry, too drunk or just plain Billy-No-Mates, Fast-Food Loser consoles himself with a solitary meal of fat-saturated comfort food in a brightly lit burger franchise, at this hour frequented by office cleaners, people of no fixed abode and other unfortunate losers in club life. Busying himself with one-handed imaginary texting so as not to look too sad, his face lights up when a real text is received; disappointingly it turns out to be another M40 traffic roadworks update. It is not unusual for *III-Fatus* to have ingested 'disco biscuits' earlier in the evening, explaining an uncontrollable foot tapping to the restaurant's normally paralysing mix of easy-listening bossa nova over the PA. Prefers to dine near an emergency exit; useful for when the directional club outfit attracts unwanted attention from kids armed with milkshake-straw peashooters and chewed-up napkins.

'Sorry sir, no flashing cyberdog t-shirts tonight'

Completes the Shrek 2 Happy Meal collection tonight. For the second time

Snake high score: 990

● Cleaner *Detergum Delectae*

The removal of foul, post-club detritus from a discotheque's toilets, floors and walls is an unenviable task, but Cleaner's iron constitution and disregard for attention to detail make the job appear trivial. A mother of four hailing from somewhere within the former eastern block, Cleaner's lack of knowledge regarding basic wage structures endears her to venue owners who sanitise their premises for the price of a bottle of Freixenet. Though never having attended, let alone run a western discotheque, Cleaner is keen to apportion advice on such matters (Why music all same please? Why women all look like men?). Postbox-red lipstick and corkscrew titanium hair is unnaturally resistant to the leadmelting fumes of stale alcohol and industrial-strength bleach. Dropped off and picked up by a blacked-out Lexus saloon. Don't ask.

To supplement breadline income, Cleaner meticulously separates two-ply toilet tissue rolls to create double the stock. Excess is sold on for pure profit at the local car boot sale.

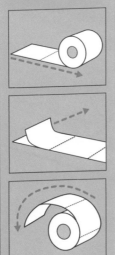

Sleeps through the entire shift

Lost stashes found on the floor: hoovered up for immediate resale on the black market

Third-hand Slovakian work gear: unknowingly the apex of 2006 spring/ summer chic

DEVIL'S DANDRUFF

Business savvy: charges more per mile than Concorde and still gets stroppy if you don't leave a tip

In-car air freshener aroma: stale Toilet Duck

● Illegal Minicab Driver *Fifteen Poundus*

To be found hunting in packs outside busy night spots, repeating the distinctive cry 'Minicab, minicab', *Fifteen Poundus* is a rare breed in that it possesses none of the primary skills essential to the job in hand, i.e. Highway Code basics, aural understanding, or civilian safety and directional awareness. These shortcomings are, however, made up for in chipper enthusiasm, a devotion to breakneck speed and an ability to judge passengers' musical moods (uptempo Fela Kuti for revellers, downtempo Fela Kuti for rowing passengers, Phil Collins for lovers). Considering the extortionate fares he charges, *Fifteen Poundus* could well afford to buy a vehicle produced this side of the 1970s, but instead prefers the blue plastic charm of the trusty Nissan Sunny, the interior of which is adorned by hanging glamour girl charms, beaded seat covers and empty bottles of Strongbow Super. Not to be confused with Random Lone Driving Male, the borderline kerb crawler who gives lifts for cash on the way home from the 24-hour snooker hall.

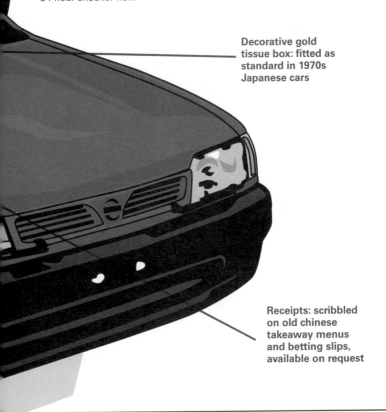

Decorative gold tissue box: fitted as standard in 1970s Japanese cars

Receipts: scribbled on old chinese takeaway menus and betting slips, available on request

DEVIL'S DANDRUFF

Will loudly proclaim 'I haven't pissed myself – I just spilt my drink' every stop

Least popular seats in the house

Self imagined irrepressible sexual allure

Saved for later

Enjoys using the aisle to brush up on his soccer skills

● **Nightbus Comedian** *Humorous Minimus*

The post-club nightbus journey home is a crushingly tedious and drawn out experience for the majority of clubbers. Countless stops, bizarre diversions, the driver refusing to start the bus again until someone stops trying to play 'Axel F' on the bell – all depressingly familiar scenarios to anyone too skint to afford a taxi. It is during this excruciatingly dull excursion that one encounters *Humorous Minimus*, a heavily intoxicated species that is loud of mouth and short of wit. While *Humorous'* jocular antics seem at first a welcome reprise from the usual drudgery, his unique comedy stylings soon tire. Having discovered a new joke that evening (such as 'Did you know Jeremy Beadle's got a massive cock? But then again on the other hand it's quite small') this will be loudly aired to fellow passengers at an opportune moment. Any murmurs of appreciation will unleash a non-stop stand up routine consisting of the same joke repeated ad nauseam at louder and louder volumes. Eventually a fellow traveller will snap, threatening the creature with the infliction of low level violence. At this point *Humorous* will retreat and spend the rest of the journey in silence, save only for unleashing a unintelligible torrent of abuse at his tormentor once they are safely outside the doors of the bus.

FAVOURITE ACTIVITIES

★ *Shouting 'You Are The Weakest Link – GOODBYE' to every single person who leaves the bus.*

★ *Loudly playing a shit mobile ring tone over and over again while laughing to himself.*

★ *Unsuccessfully offering his can of hi-strength lo-cost lager to anyone within spilling distance*

DEVIL'S DANDRUFF

● Late Night Petrol Station Attendant *Abusea Spongus*

Finding itself in a profession both unfulfilling and poorly paid *Abusea Spongus'* primary goal is avoiding confrontation wherever possible. Faced with an unenviable nightly deluge of drunks, stoners, thieves and travelling salesmen the species alters its techniques as experience in the field grows. The novice will immediately lock the doors and serve only through a minute hatch, forcing customers to dictate orders through glass over five centimetres thick. While at first this seems a safer option it is not long until *Abusea Spongus* realises that he has become both servant and clown.

3 For £10 Porn Bag: genital shrivelling properties of E, and ropey standard of models ensures jazz mags are discarded after one flick in neighbouring grannie's garden

Cassette/ Video Tapes: absolute dregs of Woolie's bargain bin resold to gas station. All time best seller: Jeremy Beadle's Cricketing Calamities

Rubbish Flower Bouquet: essential for spouses who were 'only popping out for one drink' and return twelve hours later with eyeballs rolling to rear of skull

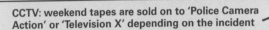

CCTV: weekend tapes are sold on to 'Police Camera Action' or 'Television X' depending on the incident

Customer procrastination over which flavour Hob Nobs to choose, the locating of a drink that doesn't exist, the reheating of a sausage roll that no-one actually wants and a quick summary of the contents of this month's issue of Razzle – all tasks *Abusea Spongus* must now undertake alone, creating both amusement for those at the front of the queue and anger for those yet to be served. Sensing defeat the doors are reluctantly unlocked and quickly the creature adapts from timid provider to weary negotiator ('please sir you have to pay for that if you are going to eat half of it') to keep lost revenue from shoplifting to a minimum.

Meek expression used to help instil guilt in borderline drunk shoplifters

Lottery Cards: for eternal optimists, habitual gamblers and poor mathematicians only

WIN WIN WIN UP TO £50,000

Ask me about my muffin meal deal' badge removed for night shift

Finger permanently hovering over Police alarm button

Brain Surgery PhD completed during the 4-6am graveyard shift

Special XXL Grab Bag

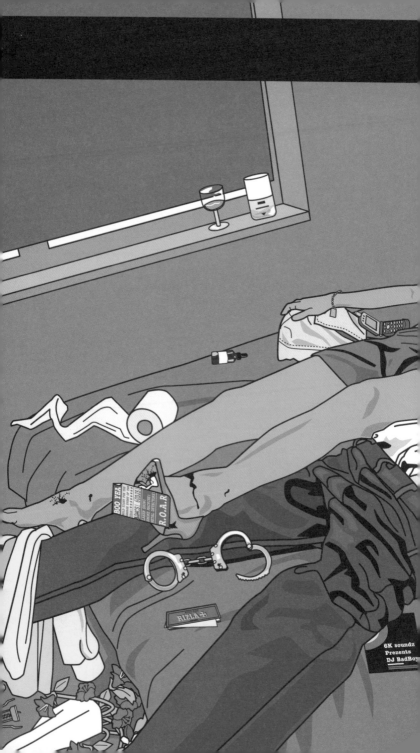